Utopias in Conflict

Comparative Studies in Religion and Society
Mark Juergensmeyer, editor

1. Redemptive Encounters: Three Modern Styles in the Hindu Tradition, by Lawrence Babb
2. Saints and Virtues, edited by John Stratton Hawley
3. Utopias in Conflict: Religion and Nationalism in Modern India, by Ainslie T. Embree

Utopias in Conflict

Religion and Nationalism in Modern India

Ainslie T. Embree

UNIVERSITY OF CALIFORNIA PRESS
BERKELEY LOS ANGELES OXFORD

University of California Press
Berkeley and Los Angeles, California

University of California Press, Ltd.
Oxford, England

Library of Congress Cataloging-in-Publication Data

Embree, Ainslie Thomas.
    Utopias in conflict : religion and nationalism in modern India / Ainslie
T. Embree.
        p.   cm. — (Comparative studies in religion and society)
    Includes bibliographical references.
    ISBN 0-520-06866-1 (alk. paper)
    1. Nationalism—India—History—20th century. 2. Nationalism—
Religious aspects. 3. India—Religion—20th century. 4. India—Politics
and government—20th century. 5. Religious pluralism—India—History—
20th century. I. Title. II. Series.
    BL2015.N26E52   1990
    322'.1'09540904—dc20   90-35275

Printed in the United States of America

1   2   3   4   5   6   7   8   9

The paper used in this publication meets the minimum requirements of
American National Standard for Information Sciences—Permanence of
Paper for Printed Library Materials, ANSI Z39.48-1984. ∞™

For S. H. E.

Contents

Preface

That the countries of Asia will occupy the position of dominance in the twenty-first century held by the North Atlantic region in the nineteenth and twentieth seems a reasonable assumption. The social and political significance of the Chinese revolution and the industrial and economic consequences of the transformations that have taken place in Japan, South Korea, and Southeast Asia can scarcely be doubted as one looks at the contemporary world. Although much less attention has been given to it, the transformation in the Indian subcontinent of the centralized imperial state of British India into the nation-states of India, Pakistan, and Bangladesh is of scarcely less significance. By reason of size alone, India would demand particular attention, but beyond sheer size is the creation of a political democracy in a territorial state with religious, ethnic, and linguistic groups so large and so distinctive, and with such separate historical experiences and memories, that elsewhere they would constitute separate nationalities, as has been the case in Europe.

The aspects of the making of a modern democratic state that I examine here follow from the assertion by religious groups and communities of their visions of a

good society. Involved in this assertion is the issue of
what representative government means in the context
of Indian society. This question has been at the forefront
of Indian life since the end of the nineteenth century,
when the demand for representative political institutions by nationalist leaders signaled the beginning of
modern politics. For most of those leaders, a fundamental requirement of good government was the expression
of the will of the people through free election. The nation was understood as an aggregation of individuals,
with the majority on any issue being the voice of the
people. This concept of the nation was rejected, however, by those who saw society as composed of groups,
not individuals, and who insisted that in a just social
order, groups, not a majority of individuals, must determine the condition of social life as expressed in laws.
For reasons that are woven into the pattern of India's
historical experience, by the beginning of modern politics at the end of the nineteenth century those groups
were defined in religious categories, and they had agen-
das for a good society legitimized and sacralized by religion. And, as is explicitly argued in chapter 3, this
means that groups so defined bring to political life a religious vocabulary in enunciating programs for realiz-
ing the good society. One of the most misleading readings of modern India characterizes religious groups as
"obscurantists" and "fundamentalists," implying that
they are opposed to modernity and change. They are, on
the contrary, agents of change who are rejecting many
of the received opinions about the nature of the liberal
state as understood in the nineteenth century.

The argument that runs throughout this book is that
the tensions generated by competing visions of the just
society, grounded in religion, have been determining

factors in the social and political life of India throughout the twentieth century. There are, of course, many
other sources of conflict within so complex and diverse
a society, but these tensions and antagonisms have been
of particular interest to me and are explored here. The
title of this book is intended to indicate that these visions of a good society, or blueprints of the future, are
integral components of the vitality and creativity of
contemporary Indian life.

Alexis de Tocqueville, the French writer who is best
known for his study of early nineteenth-century America, but who also wrote on the history of his own country, once noted how important it is for historians to "tie
together in their thoughts the past, the present and the
future." This little book is, in its own fashion, such an
attempt on a very modest scale. It is partly history in
that it is concerned with interpretations of the development of society in the past, but it is also a kind of repor-
tage because it deals with contemporary events whose
meaning and significance are far from clear. Even more
perilously, the book is occasionally about the future, because there is speculation, however tenuous and
guarded, about the directions that Indian society may
take, based upon readings and interpretations of the
past and present. The conviction that underlies this
combination of history, reporting, and speculation is
that the formation of the modern state of India, with its
commitment to government by democratic political
representation, is of primary importance in the series of
events and movements that in the past fifty years have
transformed the world system.

My many debts to other writers and scholars are acknowledged in the notes, but my gratitude to Mark
Juergensmeyer goes far beyond the notes that indicate

my borrowings from his work. He has edited my original manuscript in both a friendly and a ruthless fashion. And I would like to express my special thanks to Ilene O'Malley for many suggestions that make the book more readable.

Ainslie T. Embree
Columbia University

Acknowledgments

Portions of the essays in this volume were published in other forms, and permission to use this material is gratefully acknowledged to the following copyright holders:

J. S. Bains and R. B. Jain for "Religion, Nationalism, and Conflict," from an essay of the same name in *Contemporary Political Theory* (New Delhi: Radiant Publishers, 1980), edited by J. S. Bains and R. B. Jain; Rockefeller University Press, New York, for "The Question of Hindu Tolerance," from "Tradition and Modernization in India," in *Science and the Human Condition in India* (1968), edited by Ward Morehouse; the University of Kansas Press, Lawrence, for "The Politics of Religion in Contemporary India," from "The Social Role of Religion in Contemporary India," in *Religious Ferment in India* (1974), edited by Robert J. Miller; *The Journal of International Affairs*, for "Religious Pluralism and National Integration," from an article of the same name in vol. 27, no. 1 (1973); The Asia Society, New York, for "Muslims in a Secular Society," from "Religion and Politics," in *India Briefing* (1987), edited by Marshall Bouton; and the Graduate Theological Union, Berkeley, for "A Sikh Challenge to the Indian State," from "Locating Sikhism in Time and Place," in *Sikh Studies: Comparative Perspectives in a Changing Tradition* (1979), edited by Mark Juergensmeyer and N. Gerald Barrier.

1

Religion, Nationalism, and Conflict

In the middle of the eighteenth century Voltaire could give thanks that religious wars, "the abominable monuments to fanaticism," were over. He was looking back over the preceding century to 1648, when the Peace of Westphalia seemed to have brought to an end the era known in European history as the Age of the Wars of Religion. For a hundred years, from 1560, the major European powers had been involved in both fierce internal struggles and international wars. Many issues were involved in the wars of this century of strife, and the actors themselves were aware of the political, social, and economic implications of the struggles, but the nomenclature used to describe the rivalries was derived from religion. This was true whether it was the bitter civil war between the Catholic kings of France and the Huguenots or the rebellion of the Netherlands against Spain. Philip II of Spain, the characteristic figure of the period, expressed his political ambitions very explicitly and, no doubt sincerely, in terms of devotion to the universal Church, which he saw as under attack from rebels and heretics—for him interchangeable terms. The attempt by Mary Tudor of England to restore the old Church in conflicts that won her in Protestant history the epithet "Bloody Mary," the massacre of the Huguenots on St. Bartholomew's Day in 1572 in Paris, the destruction of hundreds of Catholic churches in the Netherlands by the Calvinists, the Spanish Inquisition— these were all religious conflicts, no matter what other elements were involved. They were also quite clearly of fundamental importance for the development of modern nations and of the new force of nationalism.

With the peace of Westphalia, the dream of a united Christendom that had for so long haunted the European imagination came to an end, to be replaced, for thinkers like Voltaire and Kant, with the vision of universal peace, of a world free from religious wars. A modern historian sums up the significance of the changes: "The Wars of Religion came to an end. While in some later conflicts, as in Hungary or in Ireland and Scotland, religion remained an issue, it was never again an important issue in the affairs of Europe as a whole."[1] Nationalism and religion, which reinforced each other in the conflicts of the seventeenth century, were replaced by nationalism alone.

Yet one of the inescapable facts of the twentieth century is the reemergence of religion in the conflicts that characterize contemporary national and international affairs. In the Middle East, in Africa, in Southeast Asia, in South Asia, and in Northern Ireland, religious affiliation seems to identify the cause of conflicts. This verbal identification does not mean that religion is the only cause of the conflicts of the area, for political, social, and economic factors are obviously present. As Wolfgang Friedman, the eminent authority on international law, put it, "A study of international problems which ignores any of these factors and elevates ideology, personal power or class domination into the single determinant of world politics oversimplifies, and thereby falsifies, as much as a study of human nature which only knows sex instinct or hunger on the one hand, or selfless devotion and love on the other."[2]

There is no doubt that to explain the conflict in Northern Ireland as simply due to Catholic-Protestant antagonism, or the division of the Indian subcontinent to Hindu-Muslim antipathy, or the warfare in Lebanon to Christian-Muslim hatred, is to use a shorthand that reduces complexity into an easily understandable journalistic account. But an equal falsification comes from the denial of the role of religious commitments in conflicts, even though such a role must be understood in terms of symbols, values, and cultural identifications and not in terms of religious doctrines. It would be absurd to argue that Catholics and Protestants kill each other in Northern Ireland because they differ over the nature of the sacrament or of the authority of the pope, but it would be equally absurd not to see that dogmas symbolize belief systems and cultural attitudes, which by accentuating the unique identities of groups may lead to conflict or exacerbate it.

This insistence on the importance of the conjunction of religion and nationalism in conflict situations does not obligate belief in religion as the primary causal factor in conflicts but rather argues that religion must be taken seriously in analyzing conflict situations where the actors identify themselves in religious terminology. This is so, even though it can be shown that it is an oversimplification, a shortcut taken by observers who do not have the inclination or the ability to probe beneath the surface.

Indicating something of the meaning that is given here to the terms *religion* and *nationalism* will suggest how they interact in historical situations, although it is not of great value to attempt very precise definitions, for their value in discourse lies, to a considerable extent, in the imprecision of their everyday usage, where they are given meaning by their context. For example, when one uses *religion* and *nationalism* in referring to conflict situations in the modern Middle East, the terms take on meaning only as one uses such modifiers as *Israeli, Jewish, Palestinian,* and *Islamic*, but they are still of vital importance for understanding social and political dynamics. In India, *Hindu* and *Muslim* are vague terms by themselves, and critics are correct who deplore their usage as self-sufficient explanations for the division of the subcontinent in 1947 into two nations; nevertheless religious allegiances are fundamental to the nationalist ideologies that dominate the political arena of the region.

Religion is used here to cover two main aspects of human behavior, which while interlocking and interdependent, can be distinguished in use. One is the personal function of religion, the other is its social role. On the level of personal, individual life, religious concerns are those that have to do with what Thomas O'Dea called "the transcendence of everyday experience in the natural environment."[3] Such transcendence of empirical experience is especially necessary where human beings confront the "breaking points" of life—issues having to do with the uncertainty of life, our powerlessness before natural forces, and the inevitable frustrations of living in a world of limitations imposed by nature and by other people.

The second function of religion has to do with social systems and social structures. It includes not only such obviously "religious" forms as rituals, priesthoods, rites of passage, myths, and belief systems but also such everyday forms as means of livelihood, food, clothing, and family relationships. This understanding of religion in terms of its function in society does not require any judgment on the truth or falsity of a religious system. What is necessary is to see that the function of religion is "to provide definition beyond the extent of our knowledge, and security beyond the guarantees of human relationships."[4]

It is often said that Hinduism and Islam are not "religions" but "ways of life," in contrast with Western society, where religion appears to be a category of experience that can be separated from other experiences. What is being expressed is a sense of the penetration of the totality of human experience by what Clifford Geertz has described as "the religious perspective."[5] The separation of religion in the West is, in fact, comparatively recent and has to do with a way of conceptualization as much as with the reality of experience. But this separation and the social reality it reflects are products of developments related to industrialization, the growth of the nation-state, nationalism, and modern science. Moreover, it is probably true that the well-defined creedal system fundamental to Christianity makes it possible to abstract the religious perspective as a belief system from its cultural context. The social origins of Christianity, as an "import" into Roman civilization and subsequently into other European and non-European cultures, also give it an entirely different historical setting. The penetration of Christianity as a discrete religion into the Roman Empire through conquest and assimilation of elements of the old society is reasonably well documented and is a central theme of the Western historical tradition.[6]

Religion understood in terms of both its role in the life of the individual and its function in society has many points of correspondence with nationalism. Discussions of nationalism frequently argue that the word is a modern one, coming into European usage for the first time early in the nineteenth century. This is, however, to equate the appearance of the word with the reality of the cluster of attitudes it connotes, leading to the assertion that such sentiments as hatred of foreign rule and desire for political freedom were unknown before the nineteenth century and, by extension, are imports into the non-Western world from Europe. What appears in nineteenth-century Europe, less a result of the French Revolution than of a long process of change and development in Western European society, is the articulation and elaboration of the concept of a rational, justifiable political state. In terms of institutional structures, nationalism is rooted in the bureaucratic, administrative, and dynastic changes of at least four hundred years of European history, and the problems it raises about the nature and validity of political authority can be traced throughout Western history. In the nineteenth century, these historical developments converged in an understanding, in Hans Kohn's words, of nationalism as the "political creed that underlies the cohesion of modern societies and legitimizes their claim to authority."[7] Loyalty to the nation was the fundamental virtue, but claim to that loyalty could only be made by rulers whose authority and legitimacy were based not on conquest or dynastic succession but on identification with the people. Part of one's own sense of identity—and a very important part—derives from one's sense of being part of a nation.

The components that make such identification possible have been variously identified: common ethnic origins; a shared culture, indicated by a common language, literary tradition, and religion; a historical record that defines the past of the nation; and a territory that circumscribes language, race, and culture. All these components comprise, however, a political creed or a statement of belief, not a description of reality. The metaphors used for the phenomenon—the "rise" of nationalism, the "growth" of nationalism—have been misleading, for they imply that nationalism is an inherent structure of historical experience and not a deliberate construct. That nationalism is, as it were, a manufactured ideology is the point Disraeli was making when he said that a nation was "a work of time and a work of art." Karl Deutsch made the same argument when he stressed that nationalism is "an attitude of mind, a pattern of attention and desires."[8] These attitudes and desires are directed to creating a sense of national identity that undergirds the modern nation-state.

Religion and nationalism have very often combined to produce social and political conflict because in certain historical situations they reinforce each other in terms of providing leadership, formulating ideologies that make change possible and desirable, and developing utopian visions of a good society. On their own, religion and nationalism each are potent stimulants to action, but they are particularly so when leaders are both religious and nationalist figures, expressing themselves in ideologies and in utopian visions that use the vocabulary of religion to define their goals for the nation. Conflicts easily, perhaps inevitably, develop when there are different religions to provide, through their leaders, different versions of reality. When religion supplies the vocabulary of nationalism, as in the Middle East, Northern Ireland, or South Asia, conflicts, even if they have their origins in economic issues, assume a religious coloration.

In emphasizing the importance of leadership in social movements, it is not necessary to become involved in the sterile controversy over the causal primacy of leaders of movements. It is extraordinarily difficult to determine to what extent the concept of "a leader" has been used to impose the category and its attendant qualities on figures in the past, for much of modern Western historical writing in its formative phase has been organized around individuals, whether dynastic figures, conquerors, politicians, or religious leaders. The polar position is to use social movements as the organizing principle for imposing order on history. But this position conflates three quite different stages of action. The first is that of individuals, who while necessarily enmeshed in the social situation of a historic moment, can be seen simply as acting out their private lives. The second is that of groups, when either by deliberate action on the part of leaders or by some response they engender without intention (as is the case with some religious figures), there emerges a group of followers who define themselves by personal loyalties to the leader. The third is that of interpretation, when historians impose order and sequence by fitting the leader and followers into coherent patterns. The working out of these three stages is seen, for example, in the career of Dayanand Saraswati, who was a potent force in North Indian life in the last quarter of the nineteenth century. His biographers are fond of describing him as "the Luther of India." This metaphor is not a very accurate reflection of Dayanand's place in Indian history, but it is witness to the necessity of examining what are perhaps the two most intractable questions regarding leadership of new movements, particularly those that challenge accepted values and attitudes.

One of these questions is what impels someone to break with the accepted religious and social norms of his or her society; the other is why people follow such a leader. The simplicity of the questions conceals the difficulties of answering them in ways that reveal the inner working of a society. In defining a conceptual framework for analyzing the nature of leadership, it has been argued that "the availability of new identities at a time when they are required is neither accidental nor unrelated to the needs of the time."[9] The argument is that disasters and catastrophes within a society weaken or make irrelevant old groups of leaders, and the way is then open for new leaders to emerge. The search for a constituency becomes in itself the means for producing change in the society, as the quest for individual meaning fuses with the need for community identification. Very often the members of this constituency come, to use Suzanne Keller's terms, from the old elites of integration and pattern-maintenance and so are able to give the new movement access to the society.[10]

In discussing the role of leadership in religious and national movements, the obvious point should not be overlooked that leadership is a meaningless concept if divorced from followers. The leader or reformer is always in search of a constituency, and, conversely, groups make leadership possible because they themselves have goals and aims that however inarticulate and inchoate, define the direction taken by the leader. Leadership is intelligible only when viewed "as the performance of those acts which help the group achieve its preferred outcomes."[11] At the same time, the leader helps in defining goals, articulating hopes and fears, offering solutions, and creating institutional structures to carry out programs. This last function is not by any means a necessary characteristic of all religious or nationalist leaders, some of whom are little concerned with institution building, which is done by the followers. Any discussion of leadership is confronted by the problem that, on the one hand, leaders uphold stability and order in society, and, on the other, they are agents of social change—reformers, revolutionaries, and prophets.

Studies of the role of leaders in religious and nationalist movements suggest that a leader may play a dual role—acting to destroy an old order, but within the new system acting to impose order and discipline. Gandhi is an example of a leader of this kind. Weber's classic analysis of the legitimacy of a leader's authority can be extended to cover both roles, for charismatic authority, traditional authority, and legal authority all blend in most religious and nationalist movements.

Questions about the working of leadership relate at once to the second aspect of the interplay of religion and nationalism, what has been called the role of religion as an "ideology of transition." The phrase is used by Thomas O'Dea in his analysis of how religion, which works to stabilize social institutions, can also become a vehicle for changing and transforming society.[12]

When new directions need to be taken in traditional societies, either because of contact with other cultures or because of internal developments, leaders, "in order to explain to themselves and to others and to justify the changes . . . develop statements of interpretations of their histories which set forth goals and render them meaningful."[13] These reinterpretations, drawing upon the past, are the ideologies that make transition to new situations possible without violent attack on existing systems. Religions, O'Dea argues, have often fulfilled the function of providing an ideology of transition. In this process, a religious system saves itself by adjusting to new demands imposed on it by society, while at the same time it saves society by bringing about needed adjustments in society. The German church historian Ernst Troeltsch saw this movement of dual compromise as the inner history of Western Christianity—the story of a search for accomodation and compromise with new forces, or "the world," and then opposition to this compromise. Although the social institutions of Indian religions and Christianity are so different as to make direct comparisons implausible, remarkably similar movements characterize Hinduism and, to a lesser extent, Indian Islam in the nineteenth century. The Brahmo Samaj, the Arya Samaj, and the work of B. G. Tilak, of Aurobindo, and of Sir Sayyid Ahmad Khan all exhibit a search for accommodation with new forces, while protesting at the same time against accomodations that have been made in the past or are being made currently by other groups. Conflict is almost an inevitability in such situations.

Emphasis on the function of religion as providing equilibrium and harmony in society can lead to very opposite conclusions about its role. Those who oppose change have often regarded religion as their principal ally. For the same reason, religion and the institutions that embody it have been bitterly hated and fiercely attacked by those who desire to reform society. Hostility, and not just toward the Church but toward religious belief itself, has been an important element in the intellectual history of the West.

The third of the three aspects of the interaction of religion and nationalism is in the development of utopian interpretations grounded in the various religious traditions. Paradoxically, the growth of utopian ideas makes the work of the leaders more complex as they attempt to use religious traditions in the creation of ideologies of transition.

"A state of mind is utopian," Karl Mannheim remarked in making a distinction between utopian and ideological states of mind, "when it is incongruous with the state of reality within which it occurs." Ideological thinking itself may, he points out, be concerned with the objects that are nonempirical and transcend any kind of provable experience, but it can still help "in the realization and maintenance of the existing order of things."[14] This was precisely the use made, for example, by various leaders in India of religion as an ideology for transition; their aim was to preserve the framework of social reality as it existed by introducing into it new ideas and new values. This was what Sir Sayyid Ahmad Khan was attempting in his theological and social reformulations. He did not aim at any major structural changes in society, but others who opposed him from within orthodoxy were concerned with creating a new Islamic society. Analogous movements within the Hindu tradition envisaged a restored Hindu society. Such visions, in Mannheim's words, are utopian because "when they pass over into conduct, they tend to shatter, either partially or wholly, the order of things prevailing at the time."[15] In the Indian context, such visions clashed not only with the prevailing order, which in political and social terms were the intrusive elements from the West, but, of more significance for the history of the subcontinent, with each other. When leaders of religious or nationalist movements look to the past in search of a golden age, they are usually in search of the future; the past becomes usable as it undergirds the future. This was the point F. L. Polak was making when he argued that "the more we examine history, the more we see that the propagation of positive, socially resonant images of the future is a determining factor in the generation of cultural patterns."[16] Such "resonant images of the future" are a common feature of religious and political movements at the end of the twentieth century. It is characteristic of utopian thinking that while it very often bases itself in a vision of a golden age in the past, its real concern is with the future for which it has a blueprint and plan.[17]

Mircea Eliade has spoken of utopian thinking as characterized by "the desire to recover religious origins, and thus a primordial history," coupled with an emphasis on the renewal of old values and structures that testifies to "the hope of a radical *renovatio*."[18] This is an excellent summary of the dynamic for the combination of religious and nationalist movements, for religion and nationalism interact in their concern for the future. Religious traditions are especially congenial to blueprints for the future, and these blueprints are infused with metaphors and values of religion. Ideologies of transition, while part of the thought of the same era, are concerned with bringing new ways of thinking and new ideas into the society; utopian thought, as defined here, wants to replace an existing society with its ideal structures. It is at this point that nationalist ideological thinking merges into religious utopian thought, with all the attendant strains and conflicts that emerge, especially when there is a rival and contradictory utopian vision.

Religion and nationalism thus intersect in the nature and function of leadership, in the construction of ideologies of transition, and in utopian visions. All three aspects of religious and nationalist movements have built into their structures not just the potentialities for conflict but, one is tempted to say, the necessity of conflict. Movements for change will be opposed by old leaders and established groups in society, but even within the movements themselves, candidates for leadership will contend with each other. Ideologies of transition will point in different directions; and utopian visions, especially as they draw upon the metaphors and vocabulary of competing religions, will lead to conflict.

Religious and nationalist movements have a further potential for conflict in that all are based upon a conviction of the possession of truth, which leads to an unwillingness to compromise. The great symbol of nationalism's assertion of its refusal to compromise is the familiar slogan, "May my country always be right, but my country right or wrong." Nationalism must of necessity subscribe to this creed. In religion the most famous symbol of the ultimate inability to compromise is the Christian assertion, to outsiders so breathtaking in its intolerance, that outside the church there is no salvation. But, properly understood, in one form or another all religious orthodoxies without exception are driven by inner logic to make such a claim. The fusing of nationalism and religion, then, can become a potent source of conflict between nations, within a state, or within a movement itself.

Several possible cases of such fusing come readily to mind. One of the most intriguing is the Taiping Rebellion in China in the nineteenth century. It appears to offer illustration and confirmation of all the areas of interaction and conflict outlined above: a leader who found a constituency in the oppressed peasantry that forced him to move in directions in which he perhaps did not intend to move; the opposition of an old and deeply entrenched class; an ideology that made use of Western religious concepts; a utopian vision that made conflict—and defeat—inevitable. In Eastern Europe, Polish nationalism and Roman Catholicism welded into a vital mix that made for national survival but also for conflict with the Communist Party. On a microscopic scale, the rise of the Mahdi in the Sudan in the late nineteenth century exhibits many of the features that result when nationalist and religious movements reinforce each other. In Ireland, rival nationalisms have coalesced with rival religions to produce a situation that defies not only political solution but also sociological analysis. In Lebanon a Christian-Muslim dichotomy marches with ideological and economic divisions that link with the nationalist antagonisms of the Arab-Israeli conflict.

But where nationalism and religion have found their most complex field of interaction is in the Indian subcontinent. The region gave birth to forms of religious experience that, while immensely rich and varied in rituals, beliefs, and social practices, nonetheless through the ages have maintained the distinctive integrating characteristics that differentiate Indian religion. These characteristics, which are briefly noted in chapter 2, are

shared in some measure by all the religions that origi-
nated in the subcontinent, whether they are subsumed
under the designations of Hinduism, Buddhism, Jainism, or even Sikhism. As the Dutch scholar Jan Gonda
has put it, this religious experience was embedded in
Indian culture, which "has long preserved the cohesion
of its provinces: religion, art, literature, and social organization."[19] One province of Indian culture that was
not successfully preserved, however, was that of political organization, for at the end of the twelfth century
political control began to pass to Turkic invaders who
brought into the region Islamic religion and Persian culture. India did not, however, become an Islamic country,
despite five centuries of political dominance, in the way
that Persia and the countries of the Middle East did. Instead, two great religions, Hinduism and Islam, with
their related cultures, shared the subcontinent. To a remarkable degree, each maintained the integrity of its
own forms of religion, art, literature, and social
organization.

How much Hindus resented the loss of control of their
political destinies to the Muslim intruders is hard to
say, for the materials on which such a judgment could
be based are fragmentary and contradictory. What is
certain is that in the nineteenth century, after the British established their political hegemony throughout the
subcontinent, many Hindu intellectuals began to reas-
sess and reinterpret Indian history and culture and its
relation to the present. A primary result of this reassess-
ment was the articulation of a nationalism that was
deeply colored by a nostalgia for the Hindu past. The
leaders of the Indian National Congress, the institution
that had such a dominant role in the making of modern
India, always insisted that they spoke for all Indians

and not for the Hindus who, reflecting the demographic reality of India, comprised the majority of its membership. An essential component of any nationalism, however, is an appeal to the past, to national roots, and Indian nationalist ideology is infused with memories of the glory that was Hindu India. Thus a fundamental aspect of the overthrow of Muslim rulers by the British was the self-confident assertion of the values of Hindu culture, including its religious component.

An assertion of religion and culture has been the bedrock that has unified many nationalist movements elsewhere in the world. But in India such an assertion, while it undoubtedly has played a similar role, was also profoundly divisive, for India was the home of a second great religious culture, that of the Islamic world. This statement does not imply the acceptance of the two-nation theory of the division of India, discussed in later chapters, but is a reminder that Indian political leaders had a variety of pasts and a variety of cultures to draw upon as they constructed nationalist ideologies. To repeat the quotation from Disraeli, a nation is a work of time and a work of art, and Muslim leaders, like their Hindu counterparts, found in religious traditions materials for ideologies of transition and utopian visions of the future. Muhammad Iqbal, perhaps the greatest Indian theorist of nationalism, argued that Islam "regarded as an ethical ideal plus a certain kind of polity," by which he meant a social structure regulated by a legal system based on Islamic principles, "has been the chief formative factor in the life-history of the Muslims of India." To give up the possibility of that polity as the basis of political life was to deny Islam, for "in Islam, God and the universe, spirit and matter, church and state, are organic to each other."[20] Out of such an interpretation of the past came the alternative nationalism that made Pakistan a political necessity.

But it was not only Muslim leaders who built a vision of the future based upon their understanding of religion. Gandhi called his utopia *Ramrajya*, the rule of Rama, which he insisted meant the rule of truth and justice for all sorts and conditions of human beings. Both Hindus and Muslims heard it, however, as a call to return India to its Hindu roots. The violent controversy (discussed in chapter 5) that erupted in 1985 when it was alleged that the birthplace of Rama had been desecrated when a mosque was built there in the sixteenth century is a fitting symbol of the conflict of two utopian visions, one based on an Islamic, the other on a Hindu, understanding of reality. The Hindu-Muslim riots of the years before independence and the massive carnage at the time of partition in 1947 are sobering witnesses to the violence evoked by a union of religion and nationalism. At the end of the twentieth century, in India as elsewhere, what has been called "the logic of religious violence"[21] continues to work itself out, a reminder of Gandhi's comment that those who said religion had nothing to do with politics knew nothing of either religion or politics.

2

The Question of Hindu Tolerance

"It is curious and rather wonderful to compare other countries with India in the matter of treatment of other religions," Jawaharlal Nehru wrote to his daughter in his letters to her from prison. In most places, he said, there was bitter intolerance and persecution of people of other faiths by the dominant religion, but in India there had been almost complete tolerance by Hinduism of the many religions that had come into the country.[1] Nehru was frequently a very harsh critic of religion, but, especially when he was speaking of the past, he returned again and again to his belief that Indian society stood in contrast to other cultures because tolerance was a fundamental aspect of Hinduism. This belief reflected the nineteenth-century view of Hinduism as a religious system peculiarly sympathetic to ideas and values outside itself; Hinduism was eclectic, choosing concepts from many sources to create an integrated world view; it was absorptive, drawing into itself other faiths, as it had with Buddhism; in a word, it was tolerant.

This emphasis on Hindu tolerance as a determining feature of Indian civilization cannot, I think, be taken as an accurate reading of Indian civilization in earlier periods, but its significance lies in its use as a hermeneutic device to serve the special social and political circumstances of nineteenth- and twentieth-century India.[2] One source of this pervasive interpretation of Indian civilization as characterized by a tolerant spirituality comes from the great German philosophers and linguists of the nineteenth century who, from a variety of often conflicting perspectives, were fascinated by India.[3] The other source is Indian nationalists, to whom the idea of Hindu tolerance and spirituality was of great value in the creation of a viable ideology that would encompass the seemingly irreconcilable belief systems of the subcontinent.

Hegel had emphasized the spiritual characteristics of Indian culture in order to show its deficiencies, as did Karl Marx and, to a lesser extent, Max Weber. To other German thinkers, however, India's spirituality, its pantheism, and its polytheism were the indicators of its cultural glory and its superiority to Christianity, Judaism, and Islam. This was the message, for example, of the book *India, What Can It Teach Us?* by Max Muller, the great Indologist, as well as of his scholarly translations from the Sanskrit classics. In a more exuberant fashion, Schopenhauer, perhaps more than anyone, popularized the idea that Indian religion was superior to the Semitic traditions. He blamed religious wars and persecutions in the West on Semitic monotheism. "To render homage to the truth," he wrote, "the fanatic crimes perpetrated in the name of religion are in reality attributable only to the adherents of monotheistic religions, that is to say, to Judaism and its two branches, Christianity and Islam. There is no question of anything resembling it among the Hindus and the Buddhists."[4] This last statement is, of course, of very dubious historicity, but Schopenhauer was expressing an understanding of Indian, that is to say, Hindu history that became pervasive in the West and, even more, among Indian intellectuals in the nineteenth and twentieth centuries. It fit in neatly with the nostalgia for the Hindu past that was a component of Indian nationalism.

The existence of so many religious groups in India, but especially of Hinduism and Islam, had become by the end of the nineteenth century the most often cited justification for opposing the movement toward an independent India with a representative form of government. Without an autocratic foreign government to maintain peace between the contending religious communities, it was argued, India would descend into bloody anarchy. On the British side, one can find endless statements of this kind, but a classic formulation came in 1905 from John Morley, the great Liberal statesman, then working to give India better government. There could be no sudden withdrawal by Great Britain, for, he asked, "How should we look in the face of the civilised world if we turned our back upon our duty and upon our own task? How could we bear the savage stings of our own conscience when, as assuredly we should, we heard through the dark distances the roar and scream of confusion and carnage in India?"[5] It was not only the British who used this kind of argument for the continuance of their rule; it was fairly common among Indians themselves. The best known statement of this point of view by an Indian came, however, from the Muslim reformer Sir Sayyid Ahmad Khan. Those who talked of a common Indian nationality and representative government were, he said, ignorant of history and present-day realities, for neither the Hindus or the Muslims would ever willingly consent to share power or be ruled by the other. "It is necessary that one should conquer the other and thrust it down. . . . Until one nation had conquered the other, peace cannot reign."[6]

Indian nationalists countered these dark visions that denied the possibility of a united, independent India with a very different interpretation of the nature of Indian culture. Indian religions, unlike those of the Semitic tradition, they argued, stressed that there were many paths leading to truth, or, in more specifically religious terms, there were many names for the same God. There was, then, no reason why religious communities could not coexist peaceably, since all shared a common goal. The heterogeneity of Indian society, far from being a weakness, was in this interpretation a source of strength, with Hinduism welcoming all insights and all truths.

With an understanding of Indian religion similar to that of Schopenhauer, S. Radhakrishnan, the philosopher who became the president of India, summarized what he regarded as the characteristic feature of Hinduism by quoting Gandhi's saying that all the great faiths of the world were equally true with his own. Tracing this attitude back to the Vedas, the most ancient texts of the Hindu tradition, Radhakrishnan said that it had also been embodied in the edicts of Asoka, the great emperor of the third century b.c. who declared that "he who does reverence to his sect while disparaging the sects of others . . . by such conduct inflicts the severest injury on his own sect." In the light of such tolerance,

Hindus welcomed Jews and Christians to India in the first and second centuries of the common era and later even the Muslims who came as invaders. Radhakrishnan recounts how the fifteenth-century Persian ambassador to a South Indian king marvelled that while Muslims regard as enemies everyone who had not accepted Islam, he was met in India with perfect toleration. "No country and no religion," Radhakrishnan concluded, "have adopted this attitude of understanding and appreciation of other faiths so persistently as India and Hinduism and its offshoot of Buddhism."[7] It was this tolerance of other religions that would make possible a united democratic India, giving the lie to those who saw violence and anarchy destroying the land without the restraining and equitable, even if autocratic, hand of British imperialism.

The emphasis on Hinduism and Indian society's tolerance of other religions and other systems of thought is, then, an essential component of Indian nationalist ideology because of the heterogeneity of the population of the subcontinent, above all because of the vast numbers of adherents of Hinduism and Islam. The task of the nationalists in creating a unifying ideology was to deny that religious differences were inevitably sources of conflict, as envisaged in the imagery of opponents such as John Morley and Sir Sayyid Ahmad Khan. The question of Hindu tolerance was, therefore, more than an academic discussion of the nature of a religious world view; momentous political issues involving the rights of minorities were being obscured by the assertion that Hinduism was uniquely tolerant and willing to absorb other systems into itself. That the Islamic community in India wanted neither to be absorbed or tolerated seems to have occurred to very few exponents of Hindu tolerance, but neither is it self-evident that Hinduism is really tolerant and absorptive in the sense that has so often been claimed.

My own understanding of Hindu civilization is that it is neither absorptive nor eclectic, for the truly astonishing factor in Indian civilization is the endurance and persistence of its style and its patterns. Indian civilization constitutes a universe in itself that differs in many fundamental ways from other major historical traditions. Its origins were certainly visible by 500 B.C., by which time its ways of thinking, style of social action, and configurations of human behavior were being formed in the physical matrix of the subcontinent. Despite internal revolutions and external invasion the fundamental patterns of thought and behavior for the overwhelming majority of the peoples of India have endured through the ages. All three great indigenous religious traditions—Hindu, Buddhist, and Jain—share in these patterns.

In short, India is heir to a way of thinking, a way of living, a way of understanding the world that is sui generis. Within Indian civilization all human questions have been asked and have been answered, and they have been answered in ways that seem to have been peculiarly satisfying to the human spirit. There appears to be no explanation for the endurance of Indian social values and patterns of ideas except that together they form a way of life that solves problems of institutional organization, that is, how people live together and interact socially, as well as those existential problems having to do with the "breaking points" of human experience, such as the fact of death, that are in the domain of religious belief.

It is the endurance of this civilization, despite its encounter with a host of other cultures and other political influences, that has led many observers to conclude that the Hindu style is absorptive, synthesizing, or tolerant. What they see is something quite different, namely, Indian civilization's ability to encapsulate other cultures and make it possible for many levels of civilization to live side by side. But encapsulation is neither toleration, absorption, nor synthesis.

On this point there is striking contrast between Hinduism and other great religious systems, especially Christianity and Islam, which are popularly supposed to be intolerant and exclusive. Christian thought and practice has always borrowed from the world in which it finds itself, showing the imprint of every cultural wind that has blown, from Hellenism to Marxism. Islamic theology, while less eclectic in modern times than Christian theology, was also born out of contact with Hellenistic philosophy. And both religions have adapted in the course of their expansion to a wide variety of cultures. Indonesian Islam, for example, is very different in its cultural manifestations from that of Saudi Arabia. Yet Hindu thought at its deepest level appears to have been remarkably little influenced by insights from outside its own geographic region or cultural milieu. This is not to say that Hinduism's elaborate philosophical structures made borrowing unnecessary. Instead, these structures, exemplified in the vast literature of the epics, philosophical texts, and the Puranas, made it possible to encapsulate a wide variety of other systems within the general context of Hindu society.

Some explanation of this phenomenon—the ability to encapsulate almost any religious or cultural entity without admitting any genuine dialogue or possibility of interaction at the most profound levels of human discourse—will be attempted as we identify the values and assumptions that underlie Indian civilization. It is these great clusters of ideas, concepts, and social practices, all inextricably interwoven by human ingenuity and the loom of history, that make Indian civilization a universe unto itself and one that encapsulates but does not synthesize.

At least five unquestioned assumptions comprise the basic fabric of classical Indian religious thought. Making this claim does not commit one to the theory that these particular concepts created Indian society, nor does it assign them a priority in chronological sequence to all other ideas. It is quite as plausible to argue that they are relatively late articulations of the inner structure of a society that had already developed in response to other pressures. But the concepts are so characteristic of the society, so pervasive at all levels of culture, so much a part of the verbal and literary tradition, that they are clues to understanding Indian culture.

The first of the five assumptions is a concept of time that stands in radical contrast to that inherited by the West from Hebraic tradition. The Hebraic, or biblical, concept of time, which in its secular versions still dominates ordinary Western thought, is a linear progression, a movement that has a beginning and will have an end. This view of time is intimately bound up with our nature and our destiny. Events within the movement of time are unique; they happen once and for all, and there is no repetition.

In the classical Indian understanding, time is thought of not in terms of linear progression but in terms of cycles that repeat themselves endlessly. Second, and this is of great significance, these cycles are conceived in terms quite beyond the scope of the human imagination. Time moves in cycles within cycles, all of immense duration, giving human history a setting not of thousands of years but of thousands of millions of years. The duration of the eras is of more importance than their cyclical quality in determining our relation to them. The greatest scientific estimates of the age of the universe, not to speak of human existence, pale into insignificance before the Indian concepts of the duration of the world and human involvement in it. Three hundred million years is the length of the fundamental cycle, but this is only a rounding out of the full story before it all begins anew.

A third characteristic of Indian time is that it has no beginning or end; there is only endless repetition of the immense cycles. Time and the universe are involved in the perpetual process of renewal and decay. Bhartrihari, the great Sanskrit poet, pays homage to the power of time in a vivid verse: "Great was the king / with his circle of courtiers, / the ladies' moon-like faces, / the host of haughty princes, the bards and their tales—but we submit to time / which swept them all from power / to the path of memory."[8] Within the cyclical movement, proud kings and all the events in which they are involved recur perpetually. Everything has been and everything will be; there is no unique event, nothing that has been that will not be again.

Finally, nothing is more indicative of the Indian view of the all-encompassing nature of time than that the gods, no less than humans, are part of the eternal cycle. This is of profound importance for all Indian mythical statements about reality. The gods, as a famous hymn in the Rig Veda puts it, are this side of creation. There is no dividing line between the human and the divine. This means there is no "holy history" that is not also

human history. There is a continuum between humanity and nature and between humanity and the gods, because all are bound in the movement of time.

The implications of the Hindu concept of time for humanity's view of its place in the cosmos are obviously
great. There is no place for the unique event, for the moment that happens only once; nor is there much likelihood of people taking too seriously their achievements
in constructing political institutions. There is not likely
to be, in short, the kind of attention to political history
that has been common in the Western world and in
China.

Closely related to this concept of time is the second
great concept of classical Indian thought—karma, the
belief that every action, whether mental or physical, of
necessity produces an appropriate result. A good action
produces good fruit, an evil action evil fruit. Karma is a
law of nature, as inexorable as the law of gravity. It has
nothing to do with a deity. Two of the great Indian systems, Jainism and Buddhism, accept the idea of karma
without question but explicitly reject the concept of a
deity.

Inextricably linked with the ideas of karma and of
time is the third and most pervasive of all Indian assumptions about the nature of the universe—belief in
rebirth or reincarnation. Because the full working out of
karma cannot find fruition in one life, the soul, or the
fundamental part of life, is reborn in some other existence. Given the concept of endless cycles of time and of
endless repetition, the possibilities for development of
the concept of rebirth are very great. Rebirth becomes
part of an endless chain of existence with karma as the
determinant force. The three concepts of time, karma,
and rebirth interweave with each other, producing the

color and pattern of Indian life, undergirding human existence. Few people who live fully within the context of Indian society, even those who are not Hindu, escape the influence of these concepts. They give meaning to human existence and answer the hard questions that life puts to humanity. Most notably, they answer for Hindus those questions that have haunted Christian thought. Why do the evil prosper? Why do the good suffer? Why is there evil?

The fourth and perhaps the most socially significant of all Indian concepts is dharma, a set of values and attitudes that can be defined as duty, or as conduct that is expected of a person in society, or as law, or as morality, or as social usage. Perhaps the best definition, however, is that it is the specific obligations that life itself imposes upon each individual. Each of us, at every moment of existence, has a duty that is defined by birth, by the most fundamental fact of human existence—being born within a social group. Involved here in a formal sense is the most ubiquitous of Indian institutions—the structure of social relationships known to Westerners as caste. In social terms, dharma means that, as a human being, everyone has obligations determined by one's position in life—in essence, by birth. No one can perform another's duties or obligations. What is right for one may be wrong for another. As one of the most famous scriptural texts puts it: "Better to do your own duty badly than another's well."[9]

This discussion of dharma leads to the fifth great assumption of Indian culture—the concept that there are many levels of truth, although all truth is one. The truth for one person may be quite different from the truth for another. For this reason it is possible, to take a familiar example, for a Hindu to declare that all religions are true, or, in the modern world, that all political ideologies are true. This is always a baffling statement that suggests intellectual confusion. What it means is that particular religious practices are true for those who believe in them.

Indian thought explicitly rejects the idea that all people can have the same perception of truth, the same understanding of reality. It seems obvious to Indian civilization that all of us do not have the same capacity for mental, moral, spiritual, or physical achievement. Here the contrast with Islam and Christianity, two religious ideologies that came into contact with Hinduism, is complete. Both those religions have at the heart of their systems an obligation to assert that all humans can share in the same vision of truth. Before this assertion Hinduism is both skeptical and affronted. The claim that a truth exists that is perceivable and available to all people and should be accepted because it alone is truth is a denial of the complex understanding of the universe built upon the five great assumptions—time, karma, rebirth, dharma, and truth itself.

At no point is Indian thought more alien to Western thought than in its assertion that there are many levels of truth, which gives to Indian civilization the characteristic that has been mistakenly understood as toleration. What follows from the assertion is not toleration; rather, all truths, all social practices, can be encapsulated within the society as long as there is willingness to accept the premise on which the encapsulation is based. The result, as was argued at the beginning of this chapter, is the creation of a universe of thought and feeling and social action complete in itself, neither admitting nor needing any external influences.

How, then, has Indian civilization reacted to alien influences? Many intruders, some with violence and some with pleading, have broken in upon the geographic region of this self-contained civilization. Or, to ask directly the question implicit in this discussion, is there any conclusion that one may draw about the incorporation of alien values and institutions in traditional Indian society?

Three historical moments illustrate very well the problems that arise when the self-contained universe of India meets external forces. The first is the coming of Islam to India—to the periphery in the eighth century and to the political center in the twelfth. For five hundred years Muslim sovereignties controlled much of India, including the great religious and cultural heartland of the Gangetic plain. What was the effect of these centuries of contact between Islamic and Hindu civilizations in terms of transference of fundamental values and attitudes from Islam to Hinduism? One is compelled to answer that there was remarkably little effect.

Such an answer immediately shows one's alignment in a great historiographical argument, for there are historians who assert that, in fact, there was much interaction. They are able to give undoubted examples in painting, architecture, dress, and manners. Much more dubious is the attempt to show relationships between Sufism and Bhakti. In the nineteenth century, when Western scholars began to study the religions of India, they were struck by the many similarities between Sufism, the Islamic expression of mystical devotion, and Bhakti, the intense communion of a Hindu devotee with a particular deity. Some of them concluded that these forms of religious ecstasy were virtually identical and that therefore one must have influenced the other. A number of Indian scholars have drawn the same conclusion, and some have argued that Sufi mysticism is a direct gift to Islam from India. Current scholarship, however, gives little credence to this interpretation. The two great systems of devotional religion can be understood in terms of their own historic developments, with their similarities being seen as responses to the needs and desires of a common human nature. Only an irenic nationalism dedicated to the proposition that there is a fundamental unity of Indian culture, including its Islamic component, can find evidence of a lasting movement from one culture to the other. The reason is fairly simple. Each civilization expressed its deepest values in a vocabulary and form that were recognized by the other as religious—that is, pertaining to those aspects of culture most carefully guarded from change. Given this, creative interchange was unlikely in those areas that both groups felt to be of greatest consequence.

The second moment of contact with an alien civilization came in the sixteenth century, when the Portuguese were active in establishing political power and supremacy in the Indian Ocean. It would have been possible at that time for Indians who were interested in European ideas to have learned from the Portuguese something of the events and movements that were transforming Europe. Yet, as far as we know, few Indians showed much interest. This lack of curiosity about European life is illustrated in a revealing example. In the sixteenth century the Portuguese introduced the printing press into India, but apparently Indians made no attempt to use the invention. The explanation is surely that the Portuguese, no less than the Indians or the Muslim intruders, articulated their ideas and values with a religious vocabulary. The questions the Portuguese asked and answered were precisely those for which satisfactory answers had long existed in Hindu civilization. Since the printing press had been introduced by the Portuguese to print catechisms for use in religious instruction, the Indians would understand it as a part of an alien and oppressive ideology. Only later would it be seen as an instrument that could be used to serve Indian, even Hindu, ends.

The third moment of contact had very different results from the first two. It came with the establishment, through the East India Company, of a Western political power in Bengal at the end of the eighteenth century. The significance of this event is not that it was the British who became the successors to the Nawabs of Bengal—themselves the successors to the Mughal empire in eastern India—but that the British came as the inheritors of political and cultural revolutions that had already profoundly modified Western life.

It cannot be emphasized too much that the meaning of British rule in India in the nineteenth century must be seen in terms of the changes taking place in the Western world during the period of British hegemony. The Enlightenment, Locke and Hume, the French Revolution, the industrial revolution, the utilitarians, the evangelical movement—all these influenced the new political arrangements that were made in India at the beginning of the nineteenth century. Unlike the Islamic peoples and the Portuguese, the British did not articulate the values and attitudes of their culture in religious terms. Instead, they used a vocabulary that made it possible for Indians to accept new ideas without any apparent infringement on the central core of the religious and cultural tradition they had so long guarded from alien intrusions.

While there may not be general acceptance of this as-

sertion of the causal significance of the religious neutrality of the British, there is fairly general agreement
among scholars that at the beginning of the nineteenth
century a marked shift in attitude took place among
many of the Hindu intelligentsia toward foreign religious and cultural ideas.[10] The centuries of Muslim political dominance had seen open hostility and quiet coexistence between Hindus and Muslims, but there is
little evidence of anything like absorption or synthesis
at the intellectual level. From the early nineteenth century, however, and continuing on to the present time,
one sees in India a hungry quest for the knowledge of
the West that is in sharp contrast to earlier attitudes.
Hindu orthodoxy had warned, for example, that one
should not travel to foreign lands, one should preserve
one's ritual purity by avoiding contact with foreigners,
and one should preserve one's own traditions from outside encroachment.

Many examples can be cited that witness to the shift
from the old exclusiveness to a new openness. Ram Mohan Roy (c. 1774–1833) is one of the most famous of the
many thinkers who interpreted Hinduism in a fashion
that would make it compatible with the new learning
and knowledge that became immediately available to
India with the British conquest of Bengal in the late
eighteenth century, but his ideas are by no means, as
they are often interpreted to be, simply a product of the
West. His mordant denunciation of idolatry in Hinduism sounds as if he had been influenced by Protestant
evangelicals, but his disapproval of idolatry preceded
his contacts with Westerners. Such condemnation of
idol worship is found frequently among Hindu religious
reformers of that era. What is different in Ram Mohan's
case is the intellectual framework in which he locates

his interpretation of Hinduism. He argues that what he called superstitious and degrading social practices, such as idol worship and the status of women in Indian society, were not reflections of true Hinduism; on the contrary, they were aberrant corruptions that had entered into the society, partly through previous foreign conquests. Original Hinduism was a pure, tolerant monotheism, which, if his fellow countrymen would return to it, would permit India to appropriate the useful learning of the West for its own advantage. By useful learning he meant, "Mathematics, Natural Philosophy, Chemistry, Anatomy, and other useful works which the Natives of Europe have carried to a degree of perfection that has raised them above the inhabitants of other parts of the world."[11] Out of this contact between Hinduism and the West would come a revived society.

Ram Mohan's concept of a tolerant Hinduism to which it would be possible to return as the basis for a new political and social order in India was immensely appealing to a later generation. One often finds an awareness, however, that such a return will not be easy, for the tolerance of true Hinduism may be obstructed by later accretions. Rabindranath Tagore, modern India's most famous poet, expressed this in 1926 when he wrote that to know the true India, one had to travel to the past "when she realized her soul, . . . when she revealed her being in a radiant magnanimity which illumined the eastern horizon." Now, however, she has withdrawn herself "into a miserly pride of exclusiveness, into a poverty of mind . . . that has lost its light and has no message to the pilgrims of the future."[12] Nehru, too, had a sense of misgiving for having praised the tolerance of Hinduism in contrast to other religions, since he also believed that Hinduism had also gone far-

ther than any other religion in perpetuating a rigid social system that prevented the penetration of new ideas
and values.[13] An even more pessimistic reading comes
from Nirad Chaudhuri in his classic *Autobiography of an
Unknown Indian*. Like Tagore, he was a spiritual descen-
dant of Ram Mohan's movement, the Brahmo Samaj,
but he argues that the dream of creating a synthesis of
Indian and Western culture, based on the ideal of Hindu
tolerance, was doomed from the beginning. "Hinduism
has an uncanny sense of what threatens it. No plausible
assurances, no euphemism, no disguise can put its ever-
alert instinct of self-preservation off its guard." It was
inconceivable, then, that any genuine transfer of ideas
and values could take place, despite the plea of reformers like Ram Mohan that their teachings were based on
the most revered of Hindu scriptures.[14]

This brings us back to the question of whether the
characteristic attitudes of the modern West, including
its political and industrial structures, can find a ready
and compatible lodging within the context of the values
and attitudes that distinguish Indian civilization. Most
modern Indians would probably not only answer affir-
matively but also deny the question's validity. There
are, however, reasons to question the optimism that
shapes so much of the discussion of modernization and
planning in India.

In the introductory chapter of India's third five-year
plan, an attempt was made to provide philosophical un-
derpinnings for the massive schemes for modernization
of the Indian economy by relating them to the cultural
values of Indian society. The anonymous author states
that it is possible to maintain the values that have characterized Indian culture and at the same time create a
new society "through the impact of the scientific and

technological civilization of the modern world."[15] The author then evokes the magic word "synthesis"; India has the peculiar capacity to synthesize the cultural inheritances of her past with the artifacts and ideas of modern science.

The interpretation of Indian society given in this book suggests that this faith in a synthesis—born of a specific interpretation of Indian culture—may be illusory. The scientific and cultural impact of the modern world may indeed transform India. However, the transformation may be marked not by synthesis but by erosion and by decay of the traditional values and ideals of Indian culture. Such decay may, of course, be accepted with equanimity or even pleasure, but it is surely worth consideration and thought, for something quite different may happen. As in previous encounters with alien elements, Indian society may encapsulate the scientific and technological learning of the modern world. In practical terms, the result would probably be the creation of urbanized, Westernized, industrialized enclaves in the midst of a countryside still traditional, still living by the codes and values of the Indian heritage. Indeed, many observers have already discerned the appearance of such enclaves. Their emergence will surely subject India to peculiar social and political stresses. But whatever the future may bring, one can fairly confidently predict that it will not be the kind of cultural synthesis of which many speak with such wistful optimism.

3

The Politics of Religion in Contemporary India

When religion is in the news in India it is almost always bad news. Communal riots; Sikh extremists; the support of untouchability by the *sankaracharya* of Puri; the killings in Kashmir that followed the theft of the Prophet's hair; stories of human sacrifice at the laying of the foundations for a bridge in Rajasthan—these are the religious images that emerge from the press, both Indian and international.

Such phenomena have led many thoughtful observers, including those in India—even those who are by no means personally ill-disposed to religious values and customs—to conclude that the only creative role religion can play in India is to accept a self-denying ordinance, to remove itself from the political arena, where its intrusion serves only to hinder the search for social justice. A. B. Shah, one of the most interesting of Indian social critics, argued in this fashion quite explicitly: "India has enough problems to tackle apart from those created by the obscurantism of its communal parties and quasi-political groups; if religion is allowed to complicate these problems, we may as well give up all hope of creating a modern, secular democracy and a single nation out of the diverse groups constituting the people of India."[1]

This is not a new note in Indian political thought; it echoes the criticism that such very different thinkers as Rabindranath Tagore and M. N. Roy made about the direction in which Gandhi led the nationalist movement.[2] Yet surely Gandhi's assessment—partly intuitive, partly the result of shrewd social analysis—that Indian nationalism would have to be articulated in a religious vocabulary was more realistic than that of his critics. Those who pleaded for a strictly political vocabulary may have been on the side of the angels of rationality, but they were asking Indian society to be other than what it is. This is to suggest not that Indian society is in some sense peculiarly spiritual or religious in contrast to other societies but only that the vocabulary of political and social discourse in India in the modern period has been inextricably related to what, for lack of a better phrase, must be termed religious concerns. In this reality is rooted the response of the dominant religious forces in India to the political groups that are attempting to bring about rapid social change.

The conflict and tension produced by the confrontation of religious formulations of society with the agents of change have often been attributed to a headlong clash between the forces of tradition (or reaction) and those of modernity (or progress). Gunnar Myrdal, for example, has spoken of such a clash as a major motif of the unfolding Asian drama. One sees, he suggests, "a set of inner conflicts operating on people's minds: between their high-pitched aspirations and the bitter experience of a harsh reality; between the desire for change and improvement and mental reservations and inhibitions about accepting the consequences and paying the price."[3] This almost mythic vision is no doubt valid; but one should not assume that it takes the form of a collision between the defenders of traditional religion and the exponents of modernity. What is happening in India is something much more complicated and more subtle.

As a basis for considering this conflict and tension, three general observations suggest themselves. First of all, the advocates for traditional religious values are not merely defending the past, nor are they reactionary in a simplistic sense. They are, on the contrary, profoundly radical, for they, quite as much as the modernizers, have a vision of the future they intend to work for. They have their own program of change and a blueprint of the good society, however fantastic it may seem to those who do not share their premises and their concerns. The defenders of tradition are "modern," as modern in their education, in their life-styles, and certainly in their political techniques as those who identify themselves with programs of change and modernization in politics and society. Second, in advancing their programs of change, the religious groups do not come in conflict so directly or so importantly with the agents of modernity as they do with other religious groups that have competing, or alternative, visions of the good society based on other perceptions of reality. This explains both the ferocity and the increasing frequency of communal riots. And third, it seems obvious that those who care most deeply for traditional religious formulations—or, to put it another way, those whose personal identities are dependent upon such formulations—are unlikely to cooperate in furthering the social and religious change desired by

the modernizers. There has always been a curious am-
bivalence in the thinking of the modernizers on this
point. Nehru at times would speak of those who supported traditional religious life-styles as obscurantists;
at others, he would appeal for their cooperation in insti-
tuting a new social order. The modernizers never seem
to ask themselves, Why should the guardians of tradition cooperate in its destruction? Perhaps one can sum-
marize these three points by saying that the traditionalists—or the radical right, to use a more meaningful
term—are not the debris of a retreating sea of faith but
a part of the wave of the future as much as the spokesmen for modernity are.

The goals of the traditionalists can perhaps be most
clearly perceived in relation to those of the modernizers, for in reacting to the modernizers, the traditionalists tend to formulate their own view of the good society. The attitudinal changes desired by the modernizers,
and the social and political forms for institutionalizing
them, can be summed up under four headings: national
unity, social justice, political democracy, and secularism. These goals are the commonplaces of political rhetoric, of the five-year plans, of the constitution itself.
There is no need to spell out the specific content of these
goals—except to say they all entail profound changes in
the fabric of Indian society. Karl Marx argued that the
British caused the only social revolution known in Asia
(at that time) by undermining the traditional society,
which "had restrained the human mind into the small-
est possible compass, making it the unresisting tool of
superstition, enslaving it beneath traditional rules, de-
priving it of grandeur and historical energies."[4] But
Marx was premature in crediting the revolution to the
British, for it is only in our own time that this revolution

seems to be really under way, with its agents coming from within the society itself. Each of the four goals of the modernizers relates immediately to the interests of the articulate spokesmen for religion because, as already stressed, they too have their vision for the future. It is perhaps fair to say that those who may be called the spokesmen for the dominant political culture of India at the present time—the groups who hold actual political power, the heirs of the Indian National Congress, even though many have long since gone into one form or another of the opposition—are in agreement with regard to the importance of these goals, although not with regard to the mode of implementing them. It is when one turns to the other side of the equation—the traditional systems of life and thought—that the sources of tension become manifest.

There is no need to stress that since Indian religious systems are not monolithic, it is impossible to make any generalizations about their responses to social change that cannot be easily challenged. Even more than with most systems of belief, those of India display an internal fragmentation that is derived from geographical particularism as well as from historical doctrinal and intellectual developments. But the responses of Hinduism, which are obviously of primary importance, can, without too much violence being done to historical reality, be fitted into two main categories.[5] The first category of responses can be called "neo-Hinduism," a blanket term that covers numerous attempts made in the last century and a half to relate Hindu religion and culture to the pressures historically associated with the establishment of British political power. The reformers have sought to purge Hinduism of what have come to be regarded as corrupt elements by declaring, on the one hand, that they are not integral to its structures and by asserting, on the other, that all religions have a common core of truth. The ideas of many of the leaders famous in modern India's social and political life fall into this category, including those of Ram Mohan Roy, Vivekananda, Aurobindo, and, above all, Gandhi. In the neo-Hindu response to social change, which denies the importance of those outward characteristics, such as caste, that are usually regarded as definitive for Hinduism, Gandhi played a crucial role, not so much because of any particular theological subtlety in his teaching but because he made this interpretation of religion of central importance in Indian politics.

The secularism that is one of the most cherished goals of the dominant Indian political culture is derived not from modern Western political practice but from Gandhi's translation of nationalist ideals into the vocabulary of neo-Hinduism. The theological basis of Indian secularism is not a denial of the claims of religion but an assertion—one can say a profoundly dogmatic one—that all religions are true. Anything that appears to be socially harmful can be abandoned—what is left will be the kernel of truth. This is what Gandhi meant when he said, "For me, truth is God," which is very different in its implications from the Christian formula "God is truth." For Gandhi and his followers such an interpretation of religion was the answer to India's most pressing political problem—the antagonism between Hindus and Muslims—as well as to such social problems as untouchability. Secularism, in the Indian sense, is an attempt to create the basic requisite of a nationalist state, a homogeneous population.

The neo-Hindu, or Gandhian, solution will always

have an attraction for people of good will, but it carries within it seeds of conflict. Many serious and knowledgeable students of modern India have wondered if Gandhi's use of a religious vocabulary—inevitably Hindu in origin—did not in fact exacerbate the political and social relations between the Hindus and Muslims. Gandhi—and this is true for neo-Hinduism in general—by overlooking the historically determined character of culture and institutions, misunderstood the intractable nature of India's social problems, especially the basis of conflict between religious groups.[6] Neo-Hinduism, not understanding that the modern religious labels were almost accidental to the deep divisions of Indian society, supposed that if it could be demonstrated that all religions had common aims, conflict would end. One might almost say that Gandhi, who was so deeply conscious of the need for personal purity, did not take seriously the problem of the fierce passions that religious differences could arouse.

There is another factor in the neo-Hindu approach to conflict that must be noted: a seemingly complete inability to understand that Muslims and Christians, to the degree that they are committed to their faiths, find their identities in being part of a religious community. For Hinduism at the deepest level, on the other hand, salvation is ultimately individualistic, concerned with transcending the social order. The statement that outside the church there is no salvation is both abhorrent and childish to a neo-Hindu, while it must be fundamental to anyone who truly lives within the confines of the Semitic faiths. Neo-Hinduism's solution to religious pluralism is thus a denial of the basis of what to Muslims is a fundamental of their faith—the sense of community. The grimmest commentary on the irrelevance of the neo-Hindu solution is given in the bitter religious riots of recent years.

One turns, then, to the second category of responses made by Hinduism in coming to terms with the modern world: that of the groups known variously as Hindu communalists, Hindu reactionaries, or, preferably, the Hindu radical right. This response is represented institutionally by such groups as the old Jana Sangh, the Hindu Mahasabha, the Shiv Sena, and the Rashtriya Swayamsevak Sangh (RSS). They are radical, not reactionary, because the goals they formulate and the solutions they propose would as truly transform Indian society as would those of the radical left. Their literature, especially in Hindi, is filled with programs for change, however absurd these may seem to those with different ideological commitments. The Hindu radical right does not appeal to the peasants, whose religious beliefs and practices have been scarcely touched by the modern world, but appeals to those, particularly in the urban areas, who are most conscious of the pressures of change.[7] This means that the appeal of the Hindu radical right will not decrease as modernization progresses in India—as liberals hopefully assume—but will increase.

The thrust of the Hindu radical right can be seen most significantly in its attitudes toward the four major goals of the dominant political culture. These goals— national unity, social justice, democracy, and secularism—are not rejected by the radical right but transformed through redefinition. Its adherents allege that it is the dominant political groups who, through a false interpretation of the goals, are destroying India. National unity, they argue, means an integrated, homogeneous society; and this can only be found by recognizing that Indian culture and Hindu culture are synonymous terms. This means, of course, that the place of the religious minorities is at once called into question, for the essence of Islam and Christianity—the belief in salvation through membership in a collective social body—seems to be a denial of national unity. Territorial integrity, a basic concern for any modern nation-state, is also given a religious coloring, for the threat to that integrity comes from such groups as the Christian tribesmen in the northeastern hills, from Sikhs, or from *India irredenta*, Pakistan. Social justice is also given a different definition—one, the Hindu radical right would insist, that draws upon the Hindu understanding of the nature of society, not upon the alien ideas of the West. There is vagueness in programmatic details, but with the continual references to the ideal of dharma as enshrined in the concept of *varna*, the traditional fourfold class division of society, it does not take a very imaginative reading between the lines to see who will be the hewers of wood and drawers of water. As for democracy, nothing in India, as elsewhere, is more easily shaped to special needs. A quotation from a Jana Sangh newspaper suggests the tone and temper of the democracy advocated by the Hindu radical right: "In any democratic country only the majority has rights. . . . Some Muslims will get terribly disturbed after reading this . . . [but] the minority will have only the rights which the majority bestows upon them at its pleasure."[8]

Secularism is, of course, the obvious area for redefinition by the Hindu radical right, with the meaning given to it subsumed by the interpretation of the other goals of the society.[9] A succinct comment on secularism was given some years ago by M. S. Golwalkar, the best-known spokesman for the Hindu right, when he stated, "The non-Hindu people in Hindustan must adopt the Hindu culture and religion, must learn to respect and hold in reverence Hindu religion, and must entertain no ideas but those of glorification of the Hindu race and culture . . . claiming no privileges . . . not even citizens' rights."[10] Such views are not put forward as part of any party's political platform, but they are part of the rhetoric of religious appeal. Such a quotation, however extreme and perhaps atypical, reinforces the point made earlier—that the radical right does not engage in frontal attacks on modernity as much as on other religious groups. The demand for a ban on the slaughter of cows illustrates this quite neatly, for it is at once a way of embarrassing the government's devotion to secularism and a way of attacking Muslims.[11] A ban on cow slaughter would be obviously sectarian legislation, but its symbolic appeal is very considerable. The attack on Urdu in Bihar and Uttar Pradesh is defended as a movement toward national unity, but the goal is a homogeneous society characterized by the dominance of the Hindu culture.

A rather bizarre illustration of the ambiguities of secularism was provided when the *sankaracharya* of Puri, one of the most prestigious figures of Hindu orthodoxy, began making public speeches in which he stated that ritual pollution and the idea of untouchability were scripturally sanctioned. Not surprisingly, he was able to quote chapter and verse.[12] The fierce public outcry that followed indicated how sensitive a nerve he had touched. The leaders of the Jana Sangh were content to say that they had disagreed with the *acharya*'s interpretation of the *shastras*, but many spokesmen for the modernizing groups, true to the neo-Hindu approach, began earnest exercises in textual criticism to show that the scriptures, far from sanctioning untouchability, preached equality and brotherhood. They had missed the point that the *acharya* was not seeking to obstruct change; quite the contrary, as his speeches made plain, he wanted to bring about what he regarded as a change for the better, a society based on what he considered a rational view of human nature and the cosmic order.

The radical right defines itself not only in relation to neo-Hinduism but, more important in many ways, in relation to the Muslim community. The use of the word "community" is misleading in that it always carries with it a sense of cohesion and homogeneity, when in fact Islam in India is almost as fragmented as Hinduism. Many commentators correctly insist that there is no Muslim response as such in India, since Muslim society is deeply divided by linguistic, cultural, social, and regional differences. But as in the case of Hinduism, it is possible to identify two main categories of responses to the pressures of modern social and political changes, with both categories analogous to those of Hindu responses.

One is a movement of accommodation that has had rather different manifestations at different periods. In the late nineteenth century, as represented by Sir Sayyid Ahmad Khan and the Aligarh movement, this movement identified itself with a relatively cautious program of theological revisionism and a political platform that opposed the democratic implications of the Indian National Congress. Then, under the impetus of Gandhian nationalism in the 1920s and 1930s, a new variety of accommodation with both the modern world and Indian nationalism found expression in the group associated with Jamia Millia Islamia, the Muslim college in Delhi. Irenic in its approach to other faiths and dedicated to a nationalism that could contain a religious pluralism, this group, known as the Nationalist Muslims, claimed for Islamic culture a significant role in the creation of a modern nation-state. Yet, attractive as its approach is to outsiders, the reinterpretations of the Islamic role advocated by Jamia Millia Islamia did not engender a very deep response from Indian Muslims. The reasons for this are partly theological, having roots in the nature of Islam as an intellectual system, but more immediate causes for the Nationalist Muslims' failure to gain wider support are found in the political and social conditions in which the Muslim community exists in India today.

Almost all observers would agree that whether the objective situation justifies it or not, a deep sense of frustration and anxiety characterizes much of the Indian Muslim community. According to Dr. Abid Husain of Jamia Millia University, it was the Muslims of India who had to pay the heaviest price for partition and independence, "not only in the form of spiritual and mental anguish but also in that of economic depression and educational and cultural backwardness."[13] It may be argued that the condition of Indian Muslims is no worse than that of millions of other Indians located in similar interstices of the social system, but the Muslims' perception of their situation as isolated from the mainstream of national life remains. There are two aspects of this perception: the Muslims are "a remnant in their own eyes," cut off from the Islamic state many of them had supported; and because of this, they are in the eyes of the Hindu majority "a potential fifth column."[14]

Out of this situation comes the second category of Muslim response to social change, one that is analogous in many ways to that of the Hindu radical right. There are a number of Muslim groups that fall into this category, but the most important in the years after independence, both in terms of its following and the articulation of its ideas, was the Jama'at-i-Islami.[15] It was founded in 1941 by Maulana Maududi to define and defend the concept of an Islamic state, but the Jama'at did not, however, support the movement for an independent Pakistan, which its leaders regarded as un-Islamic in ideology. It remained quiescent for some years after partition. Then, amidst the increasing frustration of the Indian Islamic community, it began to gain a wider response. Like the Hindu radical right, the Jama'at accepts the general goals of the dominant political culture—national unity, social justice, democracy, and secularism—but then redefined them. The Western idea of the state comes in for special denunciation as corrupt in its very essence, for the true state must be the expression of God's guidance. The idea of re-creating an Islamic state in modern India is, from a rational point of view, wholly fanciful; but the Jama'at-i-Islami represents the politics of a despair that is beyond reasonable political calculation. The rigorous simplicity of its teaching has a potent appeal for those who, as Principal Mujeeb of Jamia Millia has put it, "are ignorant of political procedure and the facts of political life."[16]

The Muslim politics of despair was not only a response to modern pressures within a modernizing society but also a response to the vision of the future sedulously propagated by the Hindu radical right. Muslims undoubtedly overreact to this propaganda, but the Jama'at's demands underline Muslim fears and frustrations. The political expressions of the Jama'at-i-Islami became more absolute, more apocalyptic, more incapable of compromise with the secular aims of the dominant political culture. One is tempted to assume that in the Indian situation the Hindu radical right is alone responsible for the increasing violence and bloodshed of the communal riots during recent years, but there is reason for thinking that the Islamic extremists—the Muslim radical right, to maintain the analogy—have been responsible to some extent for bringing about the violence. The declaration by the Jama'at-i-Islami and other groups that salvation comes through communal solidarity and obedience to God alone suggests to the more despairing Muslims that it is better to die in a righteous cause than to live in subservience to an alien culture. That death has often been the reward for such views is shown by the increasing number of communal riots in which the majority of those killed have been Muslims.

While Hinduism and Islam inevitably claim the major share of attention in any discussion of the social role of religion in contemporary India, certain insights can be gained from at least a cursory glance at Christianity's place in what has been called the "uneasy mosaic" of Indian society. Although Christianity has had roots in India for a very long time, it has often been accused, because of confrontations between modern missionaries and such Hindu reformist groups as the Arya Samaj, of being an alien, foreign minority. Since 1947, Christians have been subjected to a considerable barrage of criticism and investigation, although this has been at the level of the states rather than the central government. The general charge, however phrased, is the one already alluded to: that Christians owe primary allegiance to a religious community, and one, furthermore, that is extraterritorial in its organization. In a number of states (such as Orissa and Madhya Pradesh) this criticism has led to laws that put obstacles in the way of conversion. To most Hindus, and perhaps to many casual Western students, such restrictions may seem just. But as an acute observer of the Indian religious scene has pointed out, such restrictions are in fact the result of the tyranny of the majority.[17] They are also a denial of secularism, for in a truly secular society change of religious affiliation presumably would not be a concern of the state. That so much is made of conversion in India is perhaps an indirect testimony to the point that the Hindu radical right and the Muslim radical right both make from their different perspectives: Indian society is fundamentally Hindu, and therefore conversion from Hinduism is an attack on national identity. "The dilemma of the Christians is the nation's predicament."[18]

The vital social role of religion in modern India is to be found, then, not in the numerous attempts at accommodation made by neo-Hindus or Islamic modernists but in the activities of groups of the Hindu and Muslim radical right, especially the Hindu ones. The vitality of the religious right is not demonstrated in an obscurantist defense of the past but through an assertion of what they regard as a better vision of the future than that offered by the forces of social and political modernization. The very rapid and sweeping advances in industrialization will not lessen the conflicts and tensions but, rather, will exacerbate them. The geographical areas of conflict have been the most modern cities—Bombay, Indore, Ahmadabad, and Jamshedpur—not the rural hinterlands. One can hazard the guess that out of the vitalities of Hinduism, and perhaps also of Islam, will come not lesser but greater confrontations as the lines are more clearly drawn in the future.

4

Religious Pluralism, National
Integration, and Scholarship

At the heart of most questions regarding the role of religion in contemporary Indian politics and society is the
issue of national integration. Strongly stated religious
affiliations were often regarded by Indian nationalists
as expressions of antinational sentiments, and they considered that the mark of India's coming of age was to
define the nation without reference to religion. When
the Indian National Congress met in 1885, the president
called it "the first National Assembly ever yet convened
in India" because it was made up of representatives of
varied castes, classes, and religious affiliations.[1] In asserting the inclusiveness of the gathering, the president
was coming to terms with the question that had already
begun to haunt the nationalist leaders and was to remain with them throughout the nationalist period: Is
India a nation?

Negative and affirmative responses have been equally
dogmatic, with qualifications seldom expressed, for the
question is so basic that it seems to require an answer

free from all ambiguities. Although exhortations on the need for unity are as commonplace in Indian political rhetoric as expressions of devotion to law and order in American politics, national integration (which in Indian usage includes both political integration and the formation of a common national identity) has tended to be regarded in India as an ascribed, rather than achieved, status. The importance attached to the subject has been demonstrated in a rather curious fashion by charges from Indian officials and Indian scholars that the research of American academics, especially social scientists, has worked to undermine and denigrate India's national integration. These charges provide a useful introduction to the problems of national integration in India.

An official comment on the American understanding of national integration appeared in a wide-ranging survey of India's international relations in the *Report* for 1971–1972 of the Ministry of External Affairs. The particular issue at the time was American policy toward the secession of Bangladesh, but the discussion illuminated one of the minor irritants in Indo-U.S. relations, namely, the interest of American scholars in Indian society. The failure of scholars to understand the social dynamics of another society is not often given as an explanation of their country's foreign policy, but this was, in effect, the conclusion reached in the assessment of American attitudes toward India. The *Report* claimed that India had used every stratagem of persuasion to get the United States administration "to respond with some human feeling to the epochal carnage in East Bengal let loose by the West Pakistan military regime" in 1971.[2] The culmination of these efforts was the November 1971 visit of Prime Minister Indira Gandhi to Washington, where, casting aside the conventional idioms of diplomacy, she appealed "directly to the heart of the human race." According to the *Report*, this appeal "drew the curious response of hardening the attitude of the United States, making their public pronouncements increasingly suave and forked. It seemed that the last trace of the most elementary justice and compassion had dried up in the U.S. Administration."[3]

This is strong language, seemingly more suited to the colorful pronouncements used at the time by Peking to excoriate the gangsterish deviations of Moscow than to a ministry with a style derived from British models.

However, the attitudes and the activities of the U.S. government—including the dispatch of an aircraft carrier, the USS *Enterprise*—were regarded as sufficient justification for plain speaking, since, as the *Report* put it, in dealing with the United States, India was "up against a double barrier." One of these was the U.S. preference for "the Nazi-type atrocities" of Pakistan's military regime rather than the policies of the Indian government. The other barrier, the really crucial one, was the complete failure of the American government "to understand the forces at work on the subcontinent and the abiding values of the Indian people."[4]

This failure was immediately linked to the political and social analyses of modern Indian life made by American academics. Despite the magnitude of the effort made by those scholars in their "lavishly equipped area studies departments," no proper understanding of the Indian subcontinent had been attained. The reason was plain: American scholars had been blinded by old colonialist theories about the nature of Indian life. The bias of their research interests, it was argued, was betrayed by their emphasis on caste, communal conflict, regional and linguistic differences, untouchability, tribalism, and, above all, religion.

A not unfriendly commentator in a leading English-language newspaper gave a sample of actual research topics of American scholars in India. His list included: the modern history of the Saraswat Brahmin caste, a comparison of tribal peasant communities in India, rapid change in a Hindu temple village, the Haridas sect, the ecology of a famine region in Bengal, and local politics in a traditional South Indian religious center.[5] Anyone familiar with the inner working of American higher education will recognize these for what they are: attempts to find something new for a dissertation and reflections of contemporary fashions, as well as a genuine interest in the dynamics of social change. But to the commentator—and to many Indian intellectuals— there were sinister implications in this American concern with aspects of Indian life generally regarded as divisive.

For Indians, the preoccupation of Americans with what Indian newspapers are fond of calling "fissiparous tendencies" indicates a denial of the success of national integration. "What intrigues many top officials," according to one commentator, "is why the Americans should insist on creating problems for everybody."[6] Or, as other Indians have put it, why did they insist in the 1950s upon writing books that asked the question, "Will India make it?" Why did they ask, "After Nehru— Who?" with the implication that India lacked capable leaders. Why do they ask, "Will India go communist?"

There is an added irony here since most of the Americans who have studied India have done so with great sympathy and many of them were optimistic in their assessments of India's future. This is true, for example, of perhaps the best-known analysis of Indian national integration, Selig Harrison's *India: The Most Dangerous Decades*.[7] The emphasis of this well-written and carefully researched book is certainly on the strife engendered by religious tensions, the demand for linguistic provinces, and the role of caste in politics; but, for most Western readers, the book was a cautiously optimistic statement, given the background of Indian politics against which it was written. For many Indian intellectuals, on the other hand, it was a prophecy of national disintegration.

Another example of American sympathy being mistaken for a perverse reading of Indian society is the Indian reaction to the strong interest of American scholars in regional phenomena as a device for studying Indian history and politics, as opposed to an interest in national phenomena.[8] Many of these scholars have identified with "their" regions in much the same fashion as anthropologists identify with "their" villages, even to the extent of permitting themselves (in what they take to be an expression of empathy) to express a regional patriotism opposed to the claims of other regions. Again, this scholarly regional focus is seen as a denial of Indian national integration and a reversion to the old British insistence that "India" was merely a congeries of nationalities.

For an understanding of the Indian response to scholarly discussion of the process of national integration, it is important to remember how sensitive a nerve is being touched. John Strachey, one of the ablest government officials of India, insisted, as did British publicists all through the nineteenth century, that "the first and most essential thing to learn about India, is that there is not, and never was an India, or even any country of India possessing, according to European ideas, any sort of unity, physical, political, social or religious."[9] Political unity, even law and order, were said to be the gifts of the West. Without the imposition of the steel frame of benevolent despotism, there would be no India.

But it was not just the imperial rulers who denied that India was a nation. Behind all discussions of national integration in modern India is the shadow of those who, from within India itself, argued that an integrated nation could not be created out of the existing government of India. The new India was, in fact, the legal successor state of the old government of India, but the leaders of the Indian National Congress had passionately wanted it to be territorially coterminous with the imperial structure that had controlled the whole subcontinent. For them, the subcontinent defined the Indian nation. It was this belief that Muhammed Ali Jinnah (1876–1948), the first governor-general of Pakistan, had called into question not from fanaticism, as often said, but from a calm assessment of the nature of Indian political and social life. He summed up his position in a letter to Gandhi in 1940, after Gandhi had argued that instances of minorities joining together showed that there was indeed a common Indian nation. Jinnah pointed out that the minorities were only combining *against* Hindus, not *for* each other: "I have no illusions in the matter, and let me say again that India is not a nation, nor a country. It is a subcontinent composed of nationalities, Hindus and Muslims being the major nations."[10] The leaders of the Indian National Congress, including Gandhi and Nehru, never really faced the truth of Jinnah's insistence that the subcontinent was multinational. The result was a territorial definition of Islamic nationalism that Jinnah is alleged to have characterized as a "moth-eaten and truncated" Pakistan, while the refusal of the Congress to admit that there was more than one nation in the subcontinent made possible the self-confident, and very nationalistic, state of India.

According to the nineteenth and early twentieth-century understanding of what constituted a nation, Strachey and Jinnah were making a valid point. Quite clearly, India possessed none of the prerequisites of nationhood, if the standards were to come from the classic nineteenth-century models of Great Britain and France, for a common language, a proudly shared historical experience, a common religious tradition, and racial homogeneity are all conspicuously lacking in India. Above all, there are the deep divisions occasioned by the presence of a massive Muslim minority in the midst of a Hindu majority. These two religions are so different in their vision of reality that only the incorrigibly optimistic can easily imagine them coexisting as self-conscious communities. Aside from theological differences, the history of the Islamic civilization in India is perceived very differently by Hindus and Muslims. Precisely those events and personalities—Aurangzeb (1658–1707) is a key example—that speak most eloquently to Islamic sentiment are often symbols of oppression to Hindus. For Hindus, Aurangzeb is a fanatic Muslim who destroyed their temples and tried to Islamicize the country; Muslims remember him for his gallant, if losing, defense of the empire. Conversely, the rich creativity of the Hindu imagination, as expressed in the plastic arts and myths of which the modern Indian is so rightly proud, may strike a pious Muslim as regrettable obscenities.

Yet, despite all the forces that should prevent its national integration, India has survived as a political system. It has weathered astonishing internal pressures, including famines and other natural disasters, as well as a war with China in 1962 that ended in a draw. Then, in 1971, it achieved the virtual defeat of its enemy, Pakistan, and the discomfiture of the United States, Pakistan's ally. There is probably not a single knowledgeable observer who does not agree that, after all this, India today is far stronger, far more integrated, far more a nation, than it was when it achieved independence. Yet, none of the forces that threatened India's integrity and unity have disappeared; all of them are at least as active as they were then. Some more sophisticated explanation is needed, therefore, for the alleged failure of foreign (specifically American) analysts to understand the process of national integration in India, and Indian social scientists are currently providing one.

The foreigners' failure, the Indians have argued, stems from the fundamental analysis of development which was created after World War II. Rajni Kothari, the political scientist, argues that this analysis enjoyed almost universal acceptance because, although formulated under American intellectual leadership, it was much the same as the model devised in the Soviet Union, even though the conceptual basis there was different. This "modernization model" began with the assumption that, since the new states were poor, their main problem was economic development. This could only be achieved by first initiating the process of modernization, which included urbanization, universal literacy, social mobility, a modern bureaucratic structure, and a managerial class. The question of national integration became crucial at this point in the analysis because it was felt that most of the new states lacked identity as a nation. Due to centrifugal tendencies that were both a consequence and a cause of this lack of integration, internal stability required a strong state. National integration, therefore, took priority over local autonomy and the rights of widespread participation in the political process. "Consolidation of central authority" became a euphemism for dictatorship, which was seen by those committed to this theory of development as an almost necessary step toward national integration. In most of the developing nations, Kothari argues, "hordes of politically and intellectually servile elites" accepted the loss of political freedom as the price of national integration.[11]

In some countries, however, leaders resisted the dominant theory of development, asserting other possibilities for nation building. Among these was India, where national integration has proceeded without recourse to dictatorship. A number of factors can be identified in India that have worked toward national integration despite the extreme centrifugal pressures inherent in the society. Some of these factors are economic: a move toward economic self-sufficiency, especially in consumer goods; indigenous production of armaments; the decentralization of industries, taking into account "the politics of scale" as well as "the economies of scale"; the curbing of concentration of wealth in a few urban areas, with the prevention of the growth of "parasitic elites." Other factors working for national integration are more purely political: the development of the institutions of participant democracy as "a mechanism for the change of elites and the availability of counter-elites" and, somewhat paradoxically, the existence of "ethnic pluralities."[12]

In treating this last point, Kothari states the problem

of national integration succinctly, if somewhat enigmatically: "to disorient local minorities from external stimuli and to remove the suspicion of the majority community about the lack of patriotism of given minority community or communities."[13] Presumably, what is meant is that minorities, primarily Muslims, have extraterritorial loyalties. The "external stimuli" is, no doubt, Pakistan; the reference is to a widely held belief that Muslims are sympathetic toward Pakistan. There is also, possibly, a reference to the Christian community, which is sometimes held to have an undue dependence upon foreign countries.

How justified are the charges of the Indian officials and scholars that the extent of national integration in India has been misunderstood and the character of the problems distorted by Western scholarship? In their charges of bias and claims for success there is, not surprisingly, the assertive hyperbole of a nationalism uneasy with its achievements. But there is more to it than that: there is a well-justified awareness that the very forces that seem so inimical to nationhood have, in fact, contributed to it. In a curious way, the bewildering complexities of Indian social life and historical experience have worked to maintain the fabric of the political structure. Those characteristic features of Indian society that are so patently divisive have apparently worked in a countervailing fashion to create a pluralistic political society, with the structural strains working to buttress each other. This assertion cannot be documented in any exhaustive fashion, but a cursory analysis of contemporary trends can suggest its validity.

By definition, a plural society does not need an underlying unity, or any commitment to a single truth, to hold people together. It needs mechanisms to make integration possible without denying those characteristics that define the essential life of its component groups. Such mechanisms are easily identifiable in modern India: the bureaucratic structure of a modern state; the control by the central government of the means of coercion and protection, that is, the army and the police; methods of rewards for cooperation, tangible in economic terms and intangible in terms of prestige; and systems of communication, including, above all, a pattern of education. These mechanisms are found, in some measure, in all modern societies; in a plural society, they provide the linkage among the different groups. Their existence makes possible "the uneasy mosaic" of India's plural society.

There are four major components of the uneasy mosaic: traditional Indian social structure (dominated by the complex and protean idea of caste); linguistic divisions; religious divisions; and finally, class divisions that have their origin in the transformation of traditional society into a modern, industrializing one. These components, divisive in isolation, are, in fact, integrative in India's plural society.

As far as traditional Indian social structure is concerned, the basic point to stress is that caste is not a system, as it is so often called, but a useful descriptive rubric covering two rather different aspects of traditional Indian society. First of all, caste implies a concept, or a theory, deeply embedded in Indian thought, of how a good society works. But, since it is a theory, one will not expect to find social practice always conforming to it any more than one will expect to find that the injunction "Thou shalt not kill" is always obeyed by Christians. What one does find in India is a web of relationships based on the fact, not the theory, that birth defines the conditions of existence and that familial and group relationships, not individual desires, are (and ought to be) the determinants of a functioning society. The significance of such relationships for a plural society is that the individual finds a primary sense of identity through the group and family, that is, through caste. The American dream speaks to the individual finding identity in a melding of culture and nation-state. There is no comparable "Indian dream," nor can there be while a community defined by familial relationships remains the primary source of personal identity. But, while the familial community probably remains the primary source of identity in India, it is not exclusively so. One can argue that the triumph of Indian nationalism came when important segments of the Indian population—important in terms of numbers and of leadership—began to find their sense of identity in the national and not just in the primordial communities. In some fashion, this change of identification happened everywhere as a concomitant of the creation of the nation-state, but the nature of traditional Indian social structure has made possible a unique plural society, with great potential for both division and integration.

The caste divisions have not, on the whole, been as divisive as many feared they would be largely because of one of the mechanisms of integration mentioned above: a modern system of education. However imperfect the educational system is in India, and its critics are legion, it has been a primary force in making possible the growth of a nation-state where the centers of loyalty and identity are multiple and often conflicting. It is possible to argue that many of the imperfections in the Indian educational system are in fact the necessary characteristics of Indian national integration. The most obvious of these is the complex compromise made in regard to Hindi as defined in the constitution as the national language but with English continuing as the medium of instruction in higher education.

The linguistic complexity of India is well known. There are at least thirteen major languages in India, seven of which are spoken by more than twenty million people each. Added to this statistic is one of overwhelming social and political significance: the link language remains English, which not only is foreign but is spoken by probably not more than five percent of the people.[14] There is no real analogy to such a situation elsewhere. While the Soviet Union, for example, has many languages, the link language is Russian. The problems posed by multilingualism are obvious and have been endlessly enumerated. How will people in different regions communicate with each other? How will the central government function? And, above all, what language will be the medium for education? The debates on these subjects have been passionate and, at times, violent. The basic presupposition in India, as elsewhere, has been that there must be a national language, used for interprovince communication and for education. A common language has seemed to be a minimum component for any definition of nationalism.

The Indian solution to the seemingly insurmountable language problem has been, in effect, to refuse to say there is one solution—for any single solution would arouse intolerable tensions. Instead there has been tacit agreement that linguistic diversity will undergird and shape the society. This agreement has been reached through a variety of improvisations and ad hoc arrangements, some made explicit in law, some not even formally recognized. First, to the old argument that India cannot be a nation because the Punjab peasant cannot speak to the Madras peasant, the answer implicitly given is that the likelihood of a Punjab peasant and a Madras peasant needing to speak to each other is remote. Should the need arise, it will be in a context where both know English or Hindi, the other link language. In other words, if people need to be bilingual they will become so; an astonishing percentage of Indians do know more than one language, at least in some fashion, for there are surely more multilingual people in India than in any other country. Second, English remains the language of the elite, that is, of the people who need to communicate with their opposite numbers from other linguistic areas and the outside world. Against all sentiment and all paradigms of nationalism this remains so, and there is every indication that the number of English-speaking people in India has greatly increased since independence. This interesting phenomenon runs counter to what most observers expected would happen. Third, education is carried on in the languages that are most useful to the regional groups and the several classes being educated. Thus children in a village school in Tamilnad will learn to read and write in Tamil. That will no doubt serve whatever needs functional literacy is supposed to serve, such as reading newspapers, instructions, and political and religious propaganda. For other classes and groups, English education will be available, providing entrance into the other world, the English-knowing, English-speaking world. It is an untidy, perhaps undemocratic solution, but India's plural society follows the stress lines of its historical and social experience. The improvisations of the language solution seem to work.

While the divisions created by language and caste are

obviously of great significance, the third component of Indian pluralism is the existence of sharply differentiated religious communities that are most often identified as the primary threats to Indian political unity, denying by their very nature the possibility of a well-functioning pluralism. As noted in chapters 2 and 3, this was an important element in the British argument against concessions that could lead to democratic, representative government, as it was in the demand by Muslim leaders for autonomy for the Muslim community. Many Western observers, including the present writer, without any special commitment to the interests of either the British rulers or the Muslims, have also tended to see conflict based on religious antagonisms as the most serious obstruction to national integration.

But over and against these easy readings of modern Indian history, is there a possibility that religious differences may be a positive, and not a destructive, force? The answer given by Indian nationalists, and one persuasive enough to find wide acceptance, was that the violent Hindu-Muslim riots that became a tragic feature of Indian life in the twentieth century were not primarily products of religious antagonisms but of two linked causes extraneous to any genuine religious sentiment. One explanation of the riots was that they were deliberately provoked by the British to make their rule appear to be indispensable for the preservation of law and order; to "divide and rule," the nationalists argued, was the British strategy. The other explanation was that the use of religion to explain the communal riots masked the reality that they were caused by economic and social exploitation that was also the product of imperialism. Nehru was perhaps the most eloquent exponent of this argument, for, especially in his younger days, he viewed religion as a relic from the past used by the imperialists and their allies in Indian society to divide one group from the other. Rid the country of the imperialists and solve the problems of economic injustice, he argued, and the old religious hatreds would disappear. The opposing interpretation is that the violence has a truly religious dimension, with bitter antagonisms rooted in the various religions' different visions of the good society and of a person's place in it. The implementation of these visions by those who believe in them with passion must inevitably lead to conflict since the visions are often utterly contradictory. Those in power in India have, on the whole, accepted the interpretation that there are no ultimate conflicts inherent in religious differences. They see the resolution of the conflicts in terms of economic and social changes, but their interim pragmatic solution has been a reinforcement of the plural society. Religious groups, it is argued, can live their own internal lives, obeying their own laws and customs while they cooperate for those national goals they share in common.

The solution agreed upon by India is the secular state. The word *secular* has special resonance in the Indian political and social consciousness. The state is religiously neutral, but *neutral* means something more than separation of church and state or that no religion is established. It means, in effect, that the state and its officials try to avoid any suggestion that they have any religious preferences. The explanation for this caution is the presence of ninety million Muslims, giving India the fourth largest Muslim population of any country in the world. There are also fifteen million Christians, a small minority, but a relatively educated and vocal one. A religiously-neutral state and religious pluralism become inevitable, with the religious component of the mosaic being not only the most complex to analyze but also probably the most likely to create grave pressures within the plural society in the future. In the 1980s, as discussed in chapter 6, the most direct challenge came from the Sikh minority.

The fourth component of Indian pluralism can be mentioned only in the most cursory fashion. Out of the process of modernization and social and political change in India in the last century have come classes that are analogous to the classes of Western society. They are products of the same forces: industrialization, political democracy, and the creation of a nation-state. Largely urban, but with powerful segments in the agricultural sector of the economy, the middle class is peculiarly significant for a number of reasons. First, though it comprises only a relatively small segment of the population—at a rough guess, no more than twenty percent—it is the segment in which social change is taking place. Second, it has effective political power. It is a matter not just of rural versus urban but of a nation within a nation. It is not, however, the two nations of Disraeli, the rich and the poor, but two nations, one modern, the other traditional.

In India, as in other developing countries, what is of greatest economic importance is the existence of "dual economies," the one based on modern methods of production and distribution, the other on traditional methods. In the "modernization model" referred to above, it used to be assumed that at least two major consequences followed from the development of a modern sector of the economy of India. One was that the new sector would infiltrate and transform the traditional economy. The other was that as a consequence of increased productivity and availability of consumer goods, including food supplies, there would be a "revolution of rising expectations." This was the cant phrase used by Western observers of the Indian scene in the early fifties. In fact neither consequence seems to have followed. To a remarkable degree, the modern economy seems to exist and develop without transforming the traditional sectors, with the result that, within India, one can identify a powerful industrial country. This industrialization has been missed by many Western observers because of their near obsession with the brute fact of Indian poverty. While the per capita figures for the overall distribution of wealth may not have altered very much, enormous changes have taken place within segments of the economy. Second, expectations do not seem to have risen in the way that the confident rhetoric of the past had assumed they would. What seems to have happened is that expectations have changed in the modernized sector, while the traditional sectors of the economy have remained relatively unchanged. Recent analyses have suggested a more sophisticated version of rising expectations, one related to the "green revolution" in agriculture, where remarkable changes have taken place not just in productivity but also in a series of social and economic relationships in important areas of the countryside.[15] The general argument is that the new agriculture has caused such dislocations in traditional relations that the dispossessed and disadvantaged will force revolutionary solutions not through rising expectations but through armed uprisings. The activities of the Sikh "terrorists" in the Punjab, of the Naxalites in Bengal, and of the tribals in Eastern India give strong support to this reading of contemporary Indian history.

Such an analysis obviously has profound implications for national integration, suggesting that the truly divisive forces in Indian society may not be the ones that have been traditionally identified—caste, language, religion, regionalism—but ones that are products of modernity. Yet these forces need not lead to the breakdown of the political order, for the resilience of the Indian state suggests that Indian society is so structured that its stresses can be used creatively. Thus it has been argued that while the existence of dual economies may very well lead to the growth of an elite that is "disoriented from indigenous society and national purpose," careful social controls can obviate this inherent threat to national integration. Land reforms, labor legislation, and redistributive taxation are mentioned as effective instruments in this process.[16] This may be an overly optimistic faith in Fabian expedients, but it also reflects a true perception of Indian life.

No one, least of all the historian, should attempt to learn anything from history, but India's extraordinary historical experience does suggest that its plural society has been more resilient to external and internal traumas than many more homogeneous societies have been. It is an instinctive awareness of this experience, however difficult it may be to delineate and quantify its factual basis, that explains the curious irritation shown by Indian officials to the writings and research on national integration by Western scholars. To simplify, perhaps to the point of caricature, any projections based on social scientists' analysis of India's future must be pessimistic. The stress lines are deep and ancient, a societal San Andreas Fault moving beneath the inexorable burden of the past. But, as this essay has suggested, political leaders in India are in effect arguing that its pattern of national integration may arise out of forces that in Western models may be divisive, but in the Indian context are integrative. This argument may be masking a radical despair—there are no solutions, therefore there are no problems. The pattern of political economic development since the transfer of power in 1947, however, seems to validate the Indian claim that analyses of national integration must be rooted in specific cultural contexts and, perhaps more important, must recognize that different societies' social goals may be distorted by definitions of national integration, which almost without exception have intellectual roots in Western European and American analyses. What we are perhaps seeing, then, in the contemporary debate in India, is the attempt to create a new basis for studying the phenomenon of national integration. This process is complicated by the fact that so much research on Indian development has been done by either foreign or foreign-trained social scientists. To make a radical shift in the aims and methods of social research may not be possible, but the attempt may provide new insights into the whole process of national integration not just in what, with our ineffable ethnocentricity, we call the "developing" countries but in the "developed" countries as well.

5

Muslims in a Secular Society

In the summer of 1987 a widely circulated publicity photograph showed the new president of India being inducted wearing what appeared to be Hindu ceremonial regalia. Shortly after, a picture appeared in which the prime minister and his cabinet were shown celebrating the fortieth anniversary of independence by making a *namaste*, the traditional obeisance made to a Hindu deity. Probably very few people saw anything the least offensive in these acts, but some Muslims argued that they were a breach of the commitment to secularism. It was pointed out that the British monarch, the constitutional model for the Indian presidency, is crowned with a vast display of Christian symbolism; but the analogy is not apt since the British monarch is precisely what the Indian president is not—the head of a national church.

It is too much to say that secularism has failed as a policy in India, although this is argued with increasing frequency, but it is reasonably clear that it has not been a satisfactory solution for the Muslim minorities for whom it was intended. The ideal of secularism enshrined in the Indian constitution and implemented by the legislative bodies and the courts is an amorphous concept at best, one open to a great deal of controversy. Laws relating to family and marriage rights are an example. The legal system makes explicit provision for the guarantee by the state of the laws relating to marriage, divorce, and inheritance for Muslims and for Christians, but not, it is important to note, for Hindus. For Hindus all such matters of personal and family law are governed by the general laws of India, passed after India became independent. Since then, however, there have been increasing demands that all Indians, as Indians, should come under a common law. Special provision for the enforcement of laws for specific religious communities is, it is argued, both a violation of the spirit of the constitution and a threat to national integrity and unity. A frivolous example is that, technically, a Muslim judge with four wives could sentence a Hindu for a bigamous marriage.

In the simplest formulation, issues involving religion and politics can be stated in terms of national unity versus religious communalism. Communalism is another Indian term that defies precise definition, but it is always used in a pejorative sense, implying that religious groups stress the importance of membership in their own group over national identity and that these groups seek their own advantage over those of other groups and of the nation as a whole. The Muslims argue, however, that the Hindus, the majority community, can equate their own interests with the national interest and see even rational claims for justice by a minority religious community as an attack on a national unity. As the historian Robert Frykenberg has put it, the concept of a "majority community" is "a metaphysical construction, an illusion which has ideological and practical dangers for India's future."[1] "National unity" thus can become a code phrase to denigrate legitimate assertions of cultural pluralism. In this fashion such innocuous abstractions as communalism and secularism become part of the terminology of conflict in India.

The Indian situation is not unique, of course. Minority groups have been differentiated by their religion, language, or ethnic origins from the larger society throughout history: one thinks of non-Han people in China, Jews in medieval Europe, Christians in the Ottoman Empire, Catholic Irish in Ulster, Arabs in Israel, blacks in America, as well as Muslims in India. Such a list indicates that the word "minority" gains its meaning by time, place, and historical context, and this is especially true for Muslim minorities in modern India. The plural form, *Muslims*, is important not only because Muslims in India, like minorities everywhere, have internal class, ethnic, and sectarian divisions but also because the approximately ninety million Muslims in India are found throughout the country, and regional differences abound. In Kashmir and some districts in Uttar Pradesh, Kerala, and other states, Muslims are the majority; in general, however, they are minorities within larger regional groups. One can therefore speak of Bengali Muslims, or Tamil Muslims, or Gujarati Muslims, indicating that the Muslims share the regional characteristics of language and customs. Some writers are inclined to stress these class, regional, and ethnic differences, rather than religion, in order to make clear that Indian Muslims do not constitute a monolithic block. While this is obviously true, overemphasis obscures a fact of fundamental importance for contemporary India, namely, that the forces of social and political life in a modern nation-state tend to give at least partial unity and cohesion to inchoate and fragmented groups.

To understand the complexity of the situation of the Muslim minority in India, it is necessary to keep in mind that during the struggle for independence the argument that national identity transcended religious identity was a basic element in the ideology of the Indian National Congress. From the earliest articulation of the nationalist demands, the argument had been made not only by the British but also by many thoughtful Indians that India was so deeply divided by Hindu-Muslim antagonism that democratic, representative government was an utterly impossible dream. To imagine India without strong, authoritarian rule was to hear, said John Morley, the great Liberal statesman, "through the dark distances the roar and scream of confusion and carnage."[2] One explanation the nationalists gave of this fear of violence between the two great religious communities was that it was deliberately fostered by the British to prevent them from uniting against foreign rule; another was that the violence was born of mistrust that could be overcome by better understanding.

As with so much else, Jawaharlal Nehru gave elegant expression to enlightened nationalist sentiment when he told the Punjab Provincial Congress in 1928 that since Hindu-Muslim antagonism was rooted in the economic exploitation fostered by imperialism, it would disappear with the coming of political independence and the creation of a just economic order:

> It is an outcome largely of anger and passion, and when we regain our tempers it will fade into noth-

ingness. It is a myth with no connection with reality, and it cannot endure. It is really the creation of our educated classes in search of office and employment. . . . What does it matter to the Muslim peasant whether a Hindu or Muslim is a judge in Lahore? Economic issues run along different lines. There is a great deal in common between the Muslim and Sikh and Hindu [landlords]: and a great deal in common between the Muslim and Sikh and Hindu peasantry, but very little in common between a Muslim peasant and a Muslim [landlord]. We must, therefore, begin to think of . . . economic issues. If we do so, the myth of communalism will automatically disappear.[3]

Nehru's words are worth quoting at length because, aside from a perhaps pardonable naivety about the strength of communalism, which by 1928 had become the accepted word for Hindu-Muslim antagonism, they seem to betray a lack of awareness that the same democratic processes involved in building the new social and political order for which he labored could work to strengthen the divisive religious forces that he very genuinely deplored. Nor did Nehru—and here he can serve as a kind of shorthand for many modern Indians—take into account that his vision of religion as a personal preference subordinate to other concerns was one that Islam specifically rejected. It was the potentialities inherent in a vision of Islam that combined with the social and political forces of modern India to produce conflicts that expressed themselves in violence and in conventional electoral politics.

To speak of conflict between the Muslim minorities and the Hindu majority forces at least a cursory reference to a very difficult question. Does the history of the

Islamic intrusion into the subcontinent make a difference in the present? Are relations colored, if not determined, by the Muslim memories of the centuries when
Muslims were the rulers of India, and, of more significance for contemporary India, are the attitudes of Hindus towards Muslims shaped by remembrance of the violence done to their culture and their civilization by
Muslim invaders? To anyone familiar with certain
interpretations of the historical experience of the subcontinent during the present century, the answer must
seem so obvious as to be beyond dispute. The comments
of Al Biruni, the great scholar who accompanied Mahmud of Ghazni on his raids into India at the beginning
of the eleventh century, are often cited as summarizing
the attitudes of Hindus throughout history toward their
Muslim conquerors. Mahmud utterly ruined the prosperity of India, Al Biruni wrote, and "the Hindus became like atoms of dust scattered in all directions. . . .
Their scattered remains cherish, of course, the most in-
veterate aversion towards all Muslims." But even without this hatred born of conquest, their religion forbids
Hindus to have any social intercourse with people of another religion. "This too renders any connection with
them quite impossible, and constitutes the widest gulf
between us and them."[4]

   Al Biruni was a scholar of extraordinary ability and
great compassion, and yet reading this passage makes
one aware of its stylistic hyberbole. The passage is not
true in any literal sense: Hinduism was not destroyed,
perhaps not even weakened, by Mahmud and his successors. That there would have been hatred of the invaders
by those directly affected by them was inevitable, but to
believe that it remained embedded in the primordial
memory of Hindus over the course of a thousand years

is to move into a realm of nationalistic mysticism where the sober historian may hesitate to venture. One can argue quite plausibly that the existence of deeply rooted hatreds and unbridgeable social chasms between Hindus and Muslims is contradicted by the centuries of coexistence of the great religious communities in the subcontinent. Both readings of history are true in that they reflect the available historical realities for constructing a past to explain and justify the present.

The fundamental reality is that, despite five centuries of Muslim rule in most of the territory that is now the republic of India, Muslims constitute only about eleven percent of the population, although, to be sure, this includes some ninety million people. Furthermore, in this territory were most of the great political and cultural centers of the Muslim rulers, such as Delhi, Agra, Hyderabad, and Bijapur. Pakistan and Bangladesh, the two South Asian nations with overwhelmingly Muslim populations, were marginal to the great Muslim kingdoms that dominated the subcontinent from the eleventh to the eighteenth century. Elsewhere in the world, as in Iran, Egypt, Syria, Central Asia, and Anatolia, Muslim conquest was followed by the eventual acceptance of Islam by the majority of the population as the old religions gave way to the dynamism of the new. Spain is an intriguing exception to the general pattern, for there the Muslims, after seven hundred years, were driven out.

If one asks, as textbooks frequently do, why Islam did not enjoy the same success in the Indian subcontinent as it did in neighboring Iran, part of the answer has to be a reminder that its success is in fact demonstrated in the existence of two of the largest Muslim nations in the world, Pakistan and Bangladesh. In what is now India, two major factors were at work in determining the religious demography of present-day India. One was the nature of Hindu society. With diffused authority located in extended familial relationships ("caste" in Western terminology), but without centralized religious insitutions or explicit creeds of the Christian variety that break more easily than they bend, Hindu society was able to yield political power without conceding cultural hegemony. The other factor in the long history of Muslim-Hindu interaction as ruler and ruled was the often quite self-conscious acceptance by Hindu subjects and Muslim rulers of the legitimacy, as it were, of the others' role. This was so not because of any doctrine of toleration but because of expediency. Not only were the Turkic chieftains who invaded the subcontinent in the twelfth century few in number and far from their native territory, but India quickly became far more important to them than Ghazna or Ghur in Afghanistan. As Muslims the chieftains acknowledged their obligation to spread Islam, but as rulers they realized that revenue collection took precedence over conversion. As far as we know, none of them were willing to jeopardize their fragile regimes, based on military occupation by small armies and the dubious allegiance of conquered Hindu rajas, by engaging in conversion by the sword of the peasant masses who paid the taxes.

The picture that emerges is of rulers, and a small ruling elite, who were Muslim by religious persuasion but whose political concern was the control of a large population, most of whom maintained their Hindu religious traditions. A chronicler's account from the very beginning of the Arab conquest in the Sind in the eighth century can serve as a paradigm of Muslim rule in India. The instructions given by the governor of Iraq to Mir Kasim, the conqueror of Sind, are unambiguous: "If anyone refuses to submit to Muslim power, slay him." This command was faithfully obeyed, and the account has stories of thousands of soldiers being put to death when they held out against the invader. But it was the military power of the conquerors to which the people were obliged to submit, not their religion. Some of the people did accept Islam, but some, the chronicler records, "showed an inclination to abide by their creed, and some having resolved upon paying tribute, held by the faith of their forefathers, but their lands were not taken from them." The artisans, the merchants, and the peasants agreed to pay taxes and were protected, while the Brahmins were entrusted with the same offices they had held before the conquest. Then, according to the chronicler, the Brahmins went out into the villages, telling the people that if they did not obey the new rulers, they would have neither property nor means of living. "But if we can escape from this dreadful whirlpool, and can save our lives and property from the power of this army, our property and our children will be safe."[5] In all this there is of course much idealization, but it is a reasonably accurate summary of the relations between the rulers and the ruled during the next thousand years. And among the ruled were not just the Hindus but, in later years, the Muslim masses as well, for there is little evidence to suggest that ordinary Muslims, whether poor peasants or urban proletariat, were any better off than their Hindu counterparts.

Conflicting images emerge, then, of the Islamic past in India. There are the glorious architectural achievements of the Muslim rulers, especially the Mughals, but there are also memories of their destruction of the products of Hindu creativity. A convenient metaphor for the meeting of cultures is provided by the ruined structures around the Qutb Minar, the great victory tower in Delhi erected to commemorate the triumph of the Islamic invaders at the end of the twelfth century. When Hindus visit the complex, they may appreciate the splendor of the great Islamic monuments, but they are also likely to be aware that Hindu temples of perhaps equal grandeur were destroyed to erect the soaring arches of the great mosque. But what of Muslims at the same site? For them it is possible, as Sayyid Ahmad Khan has testified in his great study of the monuments of Delhi, to see the complex as evidence of the triumph of the true faith over a false one. They regret not the destroyed temples but the evidence that the great structures have fallen into ruin because of the defeat of the Muslim rulers.[6] The Qutb, like most of the other great Muslim monuments in India that have fallen into decay, has become a symbol for the Muslim minorities of their own fate. Around the ruins stretches the vast sprawling city of modern Delhi, vibrant witness to a resurgent Indian culture in which Muslims have not played much part.

It was not Muslims as Muslims who had lost political power in the eighteenth century but a relatively small Muslim elite. This elite had lost its power to a variety of indigenous groups within India—Marathas, Sikhs, Jats, Rajputs—as well as to external powers, including the Afghans and, most curiously, the British in the form of a multinational enterprise, the East India Company. We speak of Muslim rule in India because there is no other convenient term to use, but the vast majority of the Muslim population did not share any more in the control of the state apparatus than did the Hindu masses. Under the Muslim dynasties many high offices were held by high-caste Hindus, while "Hindustanis," as the

Muslim converts from low-caste Hindu groups were pejoratively known, were excluded.

The Muslim masses, whether in the urban centers or in the rural areas, seem to have been converts from low Hindu castes, and conversion did not bring any change in social status for the overwhelming majority. To put the most extreme case: a Hindu untouchable through conversion becomes a Muslim untouchable (or a Christian or Buddhist one, in the case of other religions). There is of course no evidence that the bulk of the Muslim population in India came from the so-called untouchable groups, but it is important for understanding Muslim minorities today to bear in mind that most of them belonged to the poorer segments of Indian society during both the period of Muslim rule and period of British rule, as they do in independent India.

To put it another way: Muslims have always been a minority in India, even at the height of Mughal power in the seventeenth century. It does not make much sense, however, to speak of the Turkic, Afghan or Iranian groups who possessed power as minorities, but it does make sense to refer to the Muslim urban proletariat or the Muslim peasantry in Bihar as minorities, even though they were of the same religion as the ruling class. Much has been made of the fact that poor and illiterate Muslims shared many practices and customs with their Hindu neighbors, such as the worship of saints, but were excluded by their religious identification from many aspects of the culture of the Hindu majority. Here, then, is where history matters: the Muslim minorities in India today are the legatees not of the centuries of political power exercised by Turkic and other Islamic groups whose culture was largely Persian but of age-old disadvantages of an impoverished people who shared neither the dominant Hindu culture nor the high culture of the Muslim rulers. The great difference between their present status and their pre-modern status is that they now have the political power associated with democracy. This was engendered by the growth of modern forms of representative government that transformed the Muslim minorities from powerless anonymity into a potential political power. With this potentiality of power come, however, the frustrations of participating in a democratic secular state without achieving a satisfactory relationship with the dominant culture. The key to this relationship is to a very considerable extent bound up with the concepts of secularism and the secular state.

The conflicts in which the Muslim minorities are involved are inextricably linked with the commitment of Indian nationalist leaders, particularly Nehru, to secularism, a term that underwent considerable transformation as it passed from its nineteenth-century British origins to become a major component of Indian political discourse. The concept is familiar enough in Western usage, with an emphasis on life lived without religious faith. It connotes a denial of a role for religion in shaping cultural values, which has led to an attack on secularism by religious leaders in the West. Illustrations of an instinctive dislike of secularism vary from the Kulturkampf of Bismarck's Germany, when authorities of the Roman Catholic Church equated it with liberalism, to the attack on "secular humanism" by modern American fundamentalists who see it (no doubt correctly) as a covert undermining of the Christian American way of life. In India, on the other hand, the word seems to have had no pejorative connotation, and one finds few com-

parable rejections of the concept by religious spokesmen. One reason for this is that neither Hinduism nor
Islam have institutions that are fundamental to their
belief systems, whereas the church is fundamental to
Christianity in all its sectarian variations.

The more immediate reason for the acceptance of secularism as an expression of a basic commitment of Indian nationalism, however, is that it was given a definition quite different from the Western one. As is so often
the case with the vocabulary of Indian politics, it was
infused with meanings resonant of India's own cultural
and historical experience. Secularism did not imply any
disparagement of religion or rejection of the importance
of its values for society but only that no religion would
be given a special recognition by the state and that all
religions would have equal status and equal honor. Secularism in this reading meant that the numerical majority, the Hindus, would not use their power to give
Hinduism a favored place over other religions. The
adoption of secularism as a fundamental aspect of nationalist politics was intended to answer those who
feared—or hoped—that the state would favor Hindus.

While the early nationalist leaders in the late nineteenth century did not use the word *secularism,* when
they insisted that the Indian National Congress spoke
for Indians as Indians and not as Hindus, even though
the majority of them were Hindus, they were asserting
religious neutrality, not hostility or indifference. This
version of secularism was suited to the temperament of
articulate Hindu intellectuals who insisted that all religions were true and that all varieties of religious experience were pathways to the same truth. That this
Hindu understanding of truth as defined by Ram Mohan
Roy and Swami Vivekananda excluded truth as under-

stood by Muslims and by minor groups such as the Christians and possibly the Sikhs seems not to have been realized by those who espoused it.

Advocates of secularism in India always insisted, therefore, that far from being hostile to religion, they valued it, whatever its particular expression, for the contribution it could make to the well-being of society. They did not recognize that there were threats to social harmony in a policy that insisted that all religions by their nature were beneficial. This is true, judging by his public statements, even of Jawaharlal Nehru, who professed to have been influenced by Marx's analysis of society. Nehru excoriated religious groups when they supported communalism, which he saw as a major factor in producing violence in India, but, at least publicly, he did not draw the logical conclusion that religion in any form was a threat to the just social order he envisioned. Instead of attacking religion as a socially debilitating false ideology that required eradication, Nehru, like most Indian liberals and social democrats, argued for a "true" interpretation of religion over and against one that led to violence and dissension. This attempt by reformers and modernists to assert the "true" understanding of the religion was doomed to failure before the certainties and the superior knowledge of the true believer.

The role of the modern nation-state has also added to the complexity of the concept of secularism in India. The Indian nationalist leaders, at least by the 1920s, assumed that the state would be the dominant actor in all public concerns. This assumption reflected the idea of the state that had become common in the twentieth century, but the function of the Indian National Congress in the life of the nation added another dimension to it because before independence the Congress had become identified with the nation in opposition to the British government. The consequences of this identification after 1947, when the Congress became the government, have often been noted by political commentators, for it became difficult to differentiate between the party, the government, and the state. For the policy of secularism this meant that the personal religious preferences of party leaders and politicians were confused with the national culture, or, to use a related concept, that Hinduism was equated with the civic religion.

The Indian version of secularism is based not upon a rejection of transcendental values but upon almost a polar opposite view: the assumption that all religions in some fashion are true, and therefore no rational person will take offense at another's ritual. Secularism was regarded, probably correctly, as a characteristically Indian solution, based on Indian metaphysics.

The violence that broke out among the Sikhs in the Punjab in the 1980s is the most obvious demonstration of this interplay of democratic institutions and religion (and is the subject of the next chapter), but here I want to consider two incidents that also began in the 1980s in which Muslim sensitivities about their rights as a community led to passionate debates and violence. These two incidents, the Shah Bano court case and the quarrel over the Babri Mosque, inflamed public opinion in ways that make it clear that, while they appeared to be relatively minor and could have been adjudicated within the existing legal framework, the incidents touched concerns central to the position of Muslims in contemporary Indian society. While these concerns are often unfocused and inchoate, they can be identified not only in the Shah Bano and Babri Mosque incidents but also in many of the riots and communal disturbances in which Muslims have been involved in the postindependence era in India.

Perhaps the most important of these concerns of religious politics in India has to do with the nature of India's political representation. Some of the decisions that led to India's present political structure, while ensuring democracy, also made inevitable the conflicts that followed from the intertwining of religion and politics. At the beginning of the century, before a measure of representative government was instituted in India in 1909 (through the Indian Councils Act, usually known as the Morley-Minto Reforms), the great issue had been what form such representation should take. The leaders of the dominant nationalist group, the Indian National Congress, were insistent that representation, however the franchise might be defined, should not recognize any difference between Indians on the basis of religion. What they wanted, they insisted, was the establishment in India of responsible, representative government on the pattern of Great Britain and Canada, with the will of the numerical majority being the will of the people. The British answer was that Western political institutions had grown up in a particular society and could not be transferred to another one so different in its composition as India, which was not a nation but a subcontinent composed of many nations. For the vocal Muslim leadership, representative government on the Western model, as demanded by the Congress, meant the permanent subjection of the Muslim minority to the Hindu majority. They demanded separate electorates to ensure the Muslims a share of power in the new government. The 1909 act was a curious compromise in that it conceded separate electorates to the Muslims, to the intense anger of the Congress leadership, but at the same time established the principal of majority rule.

The question was insistently asked: how are the rights of minorities to be safeguarded? This is a point that had received little consideration in the nineteenth-century British liberal political thought upon which the Indians had drawn. Liberal political thinkers had been concerned with the rights of minority opinions, but the situation in India was very different. The issue was not the right of dissenting opinion and individual freedom but the enforcement by government of the customs and social practices of religious communities, including the vast corpus of law dealing with inheritance, marriage, and family relationships. Could the majority legislate for minority groups in these matters, or were the internal laws of religious groups parallel to those of the state and enforceable by it? In 1986, it was the applicability of the nation's laws about such matters as marriage, divorce, and inheritance to all its citizens, irrespective of their religion, that was challenged most notably by Muslim leaders, although some Christian groups were also involved. There appeared to be some confusion in India, as in other liberal democracies, between the concept of religious freedom, one of the most cherished rights that has emerged in the long struggle of the individual against the state, and the concept of group rights. Religious freedom, in the language of the Indian constitution, means the right to practice and propagate one's faith without hindrance from the state, but increasingly this has been interpreted to mean that the government should, in effect, support through law the customs that a community claims are basic to its internal life.

The assertion that groups have rights that cannot be challenged by the majority decision of voters as expressed through the legislature is based on the argument that the nation is an aggregate of groups, not of individuals. On one level, this is merely an interesting theoretical proposition, but that it is also an intensely practical issue of immediate political consequence was shown in 1986 when the Shah Bano case and the Muslim Women (Protection of Rights on Divorce) Bill, to which further reference will be made, aroused enormous passion both among Muslims and Hindus. In a less publicized case, but one involving the same issue of individual versus group rights, a Christian woman won the right as a daughter to share in the family inheritance along with her brothers. The argument against the legal decision was that the courts should uphold what was regarded as an essential custom of the community. The rights of a group, or in the common Indian terminology, a community, against the will of the numerical majority also has been a dominant factor in the behavior of the so-called Sikh extremists in the 1980s.

A second concern of Muslims that can make religious identity a central political concern is that in a rapidly changing society other groups are benefitting economically while they are being deliberately excluded. The economic basis for antagonism between religious and ethnic groups in India is a complex and controversial issue. During the nationalist struggle, Nehru's view that it was not religion but disparities in economic opportunities that divided Muslims and Hindus was widely shared. Imperialism and capitalism, he argued, had worked together to create Hindu-Muslim hostility, and the disappearance of imperial rule and the creation of a socialist pattern of society would lessen the economic competition on which hostility was based.

Nehru and his followers misunderstood the power of

religious identity and the difficulties of creating a society free of economic rivalries. Before independence the majority of Muslims belonged to the poorest sections of the population, but after 1947 the situation worsened as many of the better educated and more affluent Muslims, who might have provided community leadership, opted for Pakistan. Competition for jobs was felt most keenly by the poorest people, both Hindus and Muslims, and it is possible to see how in the struggle for survival it was easy to identify religious and ethnic differences as causal factors in disputes that were almost wholly economic in origin. In Moradabad in Uttar Pradesh, for example, the cause of the serious riots in the 1980s was almost certainly the growing prosperity of Muslim groups, which was seen as a threat by groups of Hindu workers and traders. A similar situation seems to have existed when riots broke out in Bombay in 1984 in a working class area; Muslims who had traditionally been at the bottom of the economic ladder were seen as making gains at the expense of Hindu working class groups.

What is reasonably clear in these situations is that religious leaders and politicians have made skillful use of the frustrations of poverty and unemployment to mobilize constituencies under the banner of religion. Perhaps the most dramatic example of this was the riots in slum areas of Delhi following the assassination of Indira Gandhi in which over two thousand Sikhs were killed. Both the victims and the killers usually came from the poorest classes, with politicians legitimizing the killings in the name of religion for their own ends.

A third concern that has to be taken into account to understand the interplay of religion and politics in India is in some ways the obverse of the second. It comprises the activities and attitudes of groups from the

Hindu community who feel that their religious and cultural traditions, which they identify with the nation, are threatened by concessions to minority communities. This has always been a factor in modern Indian politics, with the assassination of Mahatma Gandhi in 1948 being the most dramatic example of its consequences. His death was the result of the outrage of a group of nationalistic, committed Hindus to whom Gandhi seemed to be responsible for concessions that they thought threatened the integrity of the nation being made to the Muslims. Indian commentators often say this "backlash" phenomenon in politics is due to the concessions allegedly being made to Sikhs and Muslims. The time has come, they argue, for India to assert its national cultural identity, which means, in effect, its Hindu culture. A comment not infrequently heard is that the partition of India in 1947 meant that the Muslims who remained in India had chosen to become second-class citizens.

A fourth factor in the connections between religion and politics is related to the age and gender of the actors in situations of violence. The actors are not members of an older generation, schooled in traditional learning and critical of a new order that is destroying the ancient landmarks of their youth. On the contrary, one can safely make the generalization that the most vociferous and violent guardians of religion in India are young men. Only rarely do women now seem to be involved in acts of religious violence, in contrast to the notable role they played in the pre-independence freedom movement and at all levels of politics in South Asia since then. The explanation often given for the absence of women in these conflicts is that Indian women naturally eschew violence because of their traditional upbringing, but this is contradicted to some extent by events in India's own history. One of the few figures still alive in the popular memory from the great uprising in 1857 against the British was the famed Rani of Jhansi, who led her troops into battle and was killed in a last-ditch encounter. Young women, particularly in Bengal, took part in the 1930s and 1940s in revolutionary movements inspired by the Communist Party and during the Second World War formed their own unit in the Indian National Army that was organized to fight on the side of the Japanese against the British. In general, however, it is certainly true that the weight of tradition, especially among Muslims, works against women becoming involved in violent protests.

The difference in response between young women and men to violence legitimized by religion is probably explained by current social conditions that have made certain groups of young men more open to the suggestion that desired ends, including religiously defined ones, can best be obtained through violence. A few generalizations can be made about these young men: they usually live in urban areas, are often employed in relatively low-status occupations, and have some education, but feel marginal to the social and economic changes taking place around them. The cry that their religion is in danger, that their group is being overwhelmed, reinforces their frustrations and anger and turns them against those who seem responsible for their situation. It is not necessary that the young men who respond to these appeals should be piously attached to the beliefs and practices of their religious group, although very often this is so. It is certainly true of the members of the nationalistic Hindu organization the Rashtriya Swayamsevak Sangh, familiarly known as the RSS, as well as with its

Muslim counterparts, such as the Jama'at-i-Islami. But in the violence of the 1980s the best-documented example was that of the young Sikhs who were followers of Bhindranwale and who fit very well this profile of the violent guardians of religion. The peculiar role of young men in the conjunction of religion and politics, along with the other three factors noted above—the claim that groups, not individuals, should be represented in the political system; the perceived grievances of minorities; the identification of nationalism with Hindu culture—are all part of the complex mosaic of Indian life.

As far as Hindu-Muslim relations are concerned, all of these factors converged in 1986 in what was known as the Shah Bano case. This was one of those issues where the surface events conceal the reality. Reduced to its essentials, the issue was the great unfinished question of Indian political life: In a democratic system, what special concessions are to be legally guaranteed to minorities, whether ethnic, linguistic, or religious?

The Shah Bano case was almost trivial in itself, but if one were to do a word count of the Indian press in 1986, it almost certainly received more attention than any other single issue, and it had repercussions that raised fundamental questions about the nature of Indian politics. Although attention to it in the press reached a high point in 1986, the case had its obscure beginnings in 1978 when Ahmed Khan of Indore in Madhya Pradesh divorced Shah Bano, to whom he had been married for forty-three years. He gave her back the three thousand rupees (about three hundred dollars) that had been her *mehr*, or marriage settlement from her family, as required by Islamic law. All of this was commonplace enough, but what was not common was that Shah Bano, probably on the instigation of her sons, who were said to be on bad terms with their father, sued for maintenance under the Criminal Procedure Code of India. When the lower court magistrate awarded her twenty-five rupees, she appealed to a higher court, which raised the award to 180 rupees. The husband then appealed this judgment to the Supreme Court of India on the grounds that as a Muslim he had to obey the Shariat, the law of Islam, which required only that he pay her maintenance, or *iddat*, for three months. A bench of five supreme court judges ruled that under section 125 of the criminal code a husband was required to pay maintenance to a wife without means of support. Chief Justice Chandrachud did not, however, conclude his judgment with this interpretation of the code; he went on to say that this ruling of the Supreme Court was more in keeping with the Quran than the traditional interpretation by Muslims of the Shariat. He then said that the time had come for a common legal code for all Indians, irrespective of their religion.

These rather gratuitous comments by the chief justice, combined with the supreme court's ruling, which would become a precedent in similar cases, led to both violent protests in the streets and lengthy debates in Parliament and in the press. In Bombay, for example, a procession of one hundred thousand people denounced the court's verdict, while in Ahmednagar, another city in Maharashtra, a group supporting the verdict was stoned by opponents. An ironic, even if somewhat irrelevant, twist was given to the situation when Shah Bano refused to accept the alimony awarded her by the court on the grounds, as she put it, that it was against the teachings of the Shariat, since the obligations of the marriage contract for both parties ended with divorce. The imam, or head of the mosque, of Indore had explained this to her, she said, and she added a comment that summarizes the argument that the will of the religious community has primacy over that of the individual: "If the majority of the community thinks it is wrong, how can one individual be correct?" But the feisty old lady added another twist to this pious ejaculation when she gave notice that she was going back to the court to get the current value of her *mehr*; since it was three thousand rupees in 1932 when it was given, it was worth at least 120 thousand rupees now.[7]

In the debates that began in earnest in 1986 over the ruling, the lines were by no means so neatly drawn as they appeared to be in the streets. At first, when the court's ruling was criticized by Muslim religious leaders as an interference in the rights of the Muslim community, Prime Minister Rajiv Gandhi seemed to support the court's decision. This was expected, as he had been presented to the Indian public as a modern man and, moreover, as one with a special concern for the rights of women. Here surely was a case where modernity and compassion would march hand in hand, for, as a writer in a magazine put it, "an old and indigent woman, after forty-three years of marriage was being callously discarded and made to fend for herself."[8] The minister of state in the Ministry of Home Affairs, a position of high responsibility although not a cabinet post, was Arif Khan, a Muslim and therefore a suitable spokesman for the government on such an issue. He made a spirited defense of the court's decision in Parliament, and the prime minister was said to have congratulated him for his speech, which, he said, had evoked widespread enthusiasm throughout the country.[9]

Political realities, however, soon asserted themselves. Rajiv Gandhi's Congress Party depended in many constituencies on the Muslim vote, which is often said to make a decisive difference in nearly 150 seats out of a total of 542 seats in Parliament. Although this seems a high estimate, it is an indication of the importance of the Muslim vote. Muslim religious and political leaders began to make clear their opposition to the court's judgment in favor of alimony for a divorced Muslim wife and to the chief justice's claim to interpret the Quran. This, they argued, was intolerable interference in the internal life of the Muslim community. The point that the religious leaders made was that the husband had no obligation to pay maintenance because divorce had abrogated the marriage contract. This was the argument that the imam of Indore had made to Shah Bano, and undoubtedly it was one that was widely accepted by Muslims. Najma Heptullah, a Muslim woman who is deputy chairman of the Rajya Sabha, the upper house of Parliament, and the granddaughter of Maulana Azad, one of the most famous Muslim leaders of the nationalist movement, noted that among Muslims there is "no business of till death do us part"; the husband's responsibility ends with the legal termination of the marriage contract.[10]

In his original speech in defense of the supreme court's decision, Arif Khan had pursued a line of argument that many people claimed played into the hands of his critics in the same way that the chief justice's had. Not content with insisting on upholding the law of the land for all Indian citizens, he had argued that the conservative Muslim legal scholars and the religious leaders, the imams and *maulvis*, were wrong in their interpretation of the Quran and the Shariat. As sympathetic observers pointed out, such reasoning exposes the fundamental weakness of the ideology of secularism, because it accepts the argument of the religionists that the precepts of religion are truths that must be accepted. All that the religious specialists have to do to defeat the theological arguments of politicians such as Arif Khan is, first of all, to show the frequent factual errors in their expositions and, second, to assert the authority of traditional over individual interpretation.

The imams and the *maulvis* did not only have the authority of their learning on their side, they also probably had the support of the majority of the Muslim community. No opinion surveys were made, no referendums held, but a Muslim college teacher from Calcutta summed up what many people felt was true with the comment that "among a largely illiterate and socially backward Muslim community," the supreme court judgment was regarded "as a threat to Islam and to the identity of the Muslims in India."[11] Nor was it only the illiterate masses but also the Muslim middle classes, including liberal intellectuals, who saw the judgment, and the enthusiastic support it received from Hindus, as a threat to the integrity of the Muslim community. This seemed to be the clear message of a by-election in December 1985 in Kishanganj, Bihar, in which Syed Shahabuddin, the general secretary of the Janata party, defeated the Congress candidate, who was also a Muslim, by a large majority. Shahabuddin was by no means a demagogic Muslim fanatic, as his opponents in Gandhi's party were fond of picturing him, but like many educated Muslims he saw the Shah Bano case not as a controversy over the right of an aged divorcee to a minimal maintenance but as an indication that a supreme court made up of Hindus and a government dominated by Hindus would use their power to weaken further the Muslim community.

The Shah Bano case was not the only issue that aroused Hindu-Muslim antagonisms early in 1986. More dramatic, and the cause of more violence and bloodshed, but of less reasoned discussion, was the Babri Mosque affair, which became inextricably interwoven with the fears and emotions aroused by the Shah Bano decision. If the bare facts of the Shah Bano case are known and easily summarized, those relating to the Babri Mosque are not, because they involve ancient Hindu myths, actions of a Muslim invader in the early sixteenth century, and decisions in a local district court. Here it may be mentioned how central the legal system is to Indian life in general and to religious controversies in particular. The commitment to secularism is constantly undermined not only because, as noted above, judges are willing to include theological pronouncements in their judgments but because the courts are frequently asked to settle disputes between religious factions. To cite a digressive example, some years ago in Indore, Shah Bano's city, the Christian congregation became involved in a bitter dispute over the authority of the bishop. The issue was a technical one having to do with ecclesiastical governance, but the local magistrate was asked to intervene, and he responded by padlocking the church door. His justification was simple: the function of a magistrate was to prevent the violence that might have ensued. The Hindu judge is alleged to have quoted Saint Paul to the quarrelling Christians: magistrates are a terror not to the good but to the wicked.

In the Babri Mosque case, the magistrate's decision had larger ramifications, for the quarrel was between Muslims and Hindus. The violence that erupted in 1986 had its origins in 1949 when idols of Rama and Sita appeared or were placed in the Babri Mosque in Ayodhya,

Uttar Pradesh. The verbs *placed* and *appeared* are the key to the dispute. The local Muslims said that Hindu revivalists had entered the mosque and set up the idols of the Hindu deity and his consort as an act of defilement of the Muslim holy place. Local Hindus declared that the symbols of Rama, the great deity much revered in North India, had been placed there not by human agency but by the action of the god himself.

The reason for this divine action was plain to believers: the temple at Ayodhya was the birthplace of Rama. Because of the special sanctity it had for Hindus, the temple was, according to the Hindu version of events, singled out by Babur, the first of the Mughal emperors in 1526, and turned into a mosque to celebrate the victory of Islam over the idolatrous Hindus. Little is known of the attitude of the Hindu population toward the mosque, which was given Babur's name by the local inhabitants, but since it was in an area that remained in control of Muslim rulers until the nineteenth century, presumably they were not in a position to protest too violently. The situation changed, however, when modern politics gave religious identity a new importance and a new role. Local Hindu politicians, appealing to both Hindu religious feelings and anti-Muslim sentiment, joined with local religious leaders in the 1960s to demand that the mosque be restored as a temple so that they could worship in what they regarded as the birthplace of Rama. The appearance of the idols in the temple, by human or divine agency, led to clashes between the two communities, and an appeal was made in 1970 to the courts to permit Hindu worship in the building. The magistrate responded by ordering the doors of the mosque, or temple, depending on one's point of view, to be locked pending clarification of the facts. Then in February 1986, a Hindu petitioned the court at Faizabad, the district capital, to restore the temple to the Hindus and to unlock the doors so they could worship there. The judge did not adjudicate the question of restoring the temple. Instead he reported that he had not been able to find any judicial document that supported the locking of the door of the mosque and therefore the lock should be removed. The local police said that doing so would not lead to violence.[12]

There was in fact little violence in Ayodhya itself, but the report of the opening of the mosque for Hindu worship added to the uneasiness and fears that had been created already by the Shah Bano decision. And also, it must be emphasized, the unlocking of the Babri Mosque led to rejoicing on the part of many Hindus, especially those usually identified as Hindu revivalists. On one level, this was pleasure at the return of a sacred site to its proper function; on another, it was gloating over what was regarded as a defeat for Muslims. By mid-February communal rioting broke out in various parts of North India, adding to the sense shared by many careful Indian observers that this new violence, added to violence in Punjab between Sikhs and Hindus, showed that religion was threatening to destroy the fragile unity of India. Editorial after editorial echoed the somber question of one editor: "Has the nation's sensitivity been dulled to a point where most people seem to be getting conditioned to live (or die) with the fatal virus of communalism?"[13] Two incidents that occurred in the spring of 1986 illustrate the working of that virus and will be briefly noted. One, in Delhi, seems to have been directly connected with the Shah Bano decision and the Babri Mosque affair. The other, in Kashmir, does not appear to have been directly affected by the two legal decisions except insofar as they added to a climate of distrust.

Indian newspapers, both by law and by good sense, are guarded in reporting religious violence in order not to increase tension and ill will, and one often has to read between the lines to get a sense of what actually happened. On 15 February the Delhi papers reported that there had been widespread rioting in the walled city the day before. This was an indication that the trouble was related to Hindu-Muslim tensions, since it was easy to start a riot in the old city, with its narrow, winding, dead-end streets and dense population of poor Muslims and Hindus, both with bitter memories of the violence of partition (the division of British India in 1947, when hundreds of thousands of Muslims and Hindus were killed). Without quite saying so, many newspapers implied that trouble had been started by Muslims. Black flags condemning the decision of the Faizabad court to unlock the Babri Mosque were seen everywhere, it was reported, and the imam, in his Friday sermon in the great mosque, the Jama Masjid, was said to have denounced the decision. Thousands of worshippers went on a rampage as they left the mosque, stoning the police, stopping buses, breaking windows. At first the Muslims seem to be blamed, but then there is a curious sentence in one account: "The violence did not seem directed against members of any particular community."[14] This remark refers to the activity of a group that is one of the constant elements of communal riots—the *goondas*, the criminal underclass, who are for hire by politicians for the loot that they can pick up and for the pleasure that comes from violence. It may very well have been the Muslim leaders who started the riots by inflaming their followers, but politicians were ready to use goondas in the conflict for their own ends. What the rioters seemed to have in common as a target for attack, in this as in other communal riots, was the police. It is sometimes said that this happens because the police stand for law and order against the lawlessness of the mobs, but a more cynical explanation often put forward in India is that the police are a third force of violence and corruption.

In both the Shah Bano and Babri Mosque incidents, the lines of conflict were fairly clearly drawn, as far as Muslims were concerned. The legal rights of Muslims as a religious community within the Indian national state, as guaranteed by the constitution, Muslims argued, were being challenged by Hindu groups who were antagonistic to the continuance of those rights. Occasionally the question was raised by some Hindus: are Muslims really committed to being Indian citizens or do they have an extraterritorial loyalty to Pakistan, the state that destroyed the unity of India in 1947 and remains its enemy? This question took on a more strident tone in the 1980s in Kashmir, when fierce rioting by the Muslim population, the majority in the state, was aimed not just at the Hindus but at the Indian state itself. Events in Kashmir provide, therefore, an interesting contrast to the situation of Muslims in India, who insist that though they want special rights, they are loyal citizens of the Indian nation. In Kashmir, "Hindu" and "Indian" were used by militant Muslim groups as synonymous terms for what was regarded as an invading power intent on crushing the Islamic religion and culture of the Kashmiris. To the embarrassment of the Indians who have maintained a consistently anti-Israeli stance through the years, the Kashmiris compared India to Israel and themselves to the beleaguered Palestinians defending their religion against a foreign enemy. Equating Indian political control of the region with Hindu domination, a young Kashmiri woman expressed an apparently widespread attitude when in reference to the immensely popular serialization on national Indian television of the Hindu epics the *Mahabharata* and the *Ramayana*, she declared, "Their television programs are full of Hindu scriptures. Their police shoot our boys." For her, the two statements were not non sequiturs; the killing of Muslim youths was a product of Hindu culture. She urged other women to join the antigovernment, anti-Hindu movement.[15] This suggests that in Kashmir women may be willing to take a more active role in religiously inspired violence than, as argued above, has been the case elsewhere in India.

While elsewhere in India Muslims have suffered the most from Hindu-Muslim riots, in Kashmir it has been the Hindus, now a small minority, who have been the victims, at least in their own and Indian eyes. Kashmiris insist, of course, that they have been the victims of the violence of the Indian government. At the time of independence in 1947, Hindus numbered about three hundred thousand, but many of them have fled to India through the years, and they now number about seventy thousand in a population of six million Muslims. The Hindus complain of discrimination against them by the Muslim majority. They are, however, a curious minority, for the state was ruled for just over one hundred years, from 1846 to 1947, by Hindu chieftains, and the Kashmiri Hindus—almost all of whom were Brahmin—enjoyed extraordinary power in the management of the state. The Kashmiri Muslims resented them then and resented them even more when they gained a measure of political freedom in 1947. This was particularly so because they felt their control of their state was eroded by the imposition of an unpopular administration by a Delhi government that was perceived as Hindu and anti-Muslim. The result was that at the end of February 1986 bitter riots directed at the Hindu minority broke out, especially in the area of Anantnag, where a number of prosperous Hindu families were living. Explanations of the rioting covered familiar ground: stories that Hindu women had been raped in Jammu, the Hindu part of the state, which was untrue; stories that the Babri Mosque had been turned into a temple, which was partly true; and stories that the Shiv Sena, a Hindu organization dedicated to defending religion, had boasted of the victory at Babri Mosque, which was true.

The evidence of rising discontent among the Muslims convinced Gandhi's administration in 1986 that some action had to be taken not only to ensure the continued support of Muslim voters but also to prevent further outbreaks of violence. The step that the government believed would restore Muslim confidence was to introduce a bill in Parliament that effectively abrogated the precedent set by the supreme court's award of maintenance to Shah Bano. This award had been given under the provisions of section 125 of the Criminal Procedure Code, which required husbands to support their divorced wives, but the bill abrogated this for Muslims by stating that the clause did not apply to Muslim marriages. Arif Khan, the minister who a short time before had won the prime minister's approval for his defense of the court decision, resigned his office, no doubt feeling betrayed by the sudden shift on the part of the prime minister.

The proposed legislation, formally known as the Muslim Women (Protection of Rights on Divorce) Bill, took away the right of a divorced Muslim wife to receive maintenance from her husband but provided for her support by saying that it would be the duty, in the first instance, of the woman's family and relatives to support her: if they were unable to do so, she could appeal to the *waqf*, the charitable trusts maintained for pious purposes. In defense of the bill, the prime minister said it would further the secularism that was at the heart of India's strength by ensuring religious communities that they were not deprived of anything that they felt was basic to them. There was no hint in his speech that he was aware that before independence his party had made its stand on common laws and common citizenship and that a denial of the relevance of religious affiliation to nationalism had been central to its ideology.

The controversy over the Muslim Women Bill displayed in a remarkable fashion one of the most important aspects of Indian society, namely, the very high quality of literary journalism. Daily newspapers and popular weekly magazines, of which there are an astonishing number, published numerous analytical articles that were far more scholarly and penetrating in their discussion of the role of religion in society than would have been their counterparts elsewhere in the English-speaking world. This was not because Indians are more religious than people elsewhere but because editors and readers recognized that fundamental issues were being raised about the dynamics of Indian society and that the future direction of Indian society was at stake.

Attacks on the bill came swiftly and from many quarters. For many liberals, both Muslim and Hindu, the bill represented a capitulation to the forces of Islamic obscurantism, a return, as they were fond of saying, to the thirteenth century. At the same time, Hindu revivalists denounced the bill as weakening Indian unity by pandering to Muslim separatism and encouraging Muslims to put membership in their religious community above the claims of the nation. It especially angered Muslims, whether liberal or conservative, that Hindus argued that injustice was being done to Muslim women by the bill, but one of the most telling responses to this line of argument came from a non-Muslim, Madhu Kishwar, editor of *Manushi*, the most outspoken feminist journal in India.

Kishwar saw this new Hindu concern for Muslim women as a thinly veiled expression of hostility and contempt for Muslims. Not only were conservative and orthodox Muslims offended, but liberal Muslims who might have opposed the bill felt that by doing so they were making common cause with Hindu bigotry. Kishwar made an interesting comparison between this new concern and the British use in the nineteenth century of the plight of Hindu women as a symbol of the backward state of Hindu society. Such customs as the burning of widows, child marriage, and female infanticide were used, she argued, as proof that Indians could not run their own society in a civilized manner. Today, she said, Hindus cite the treatment of Muslim women as proof that Muslims are backward and that Islam is a barbaric religion.[16] That Kishwar was not far off the mark is suggested by a series of lengthy articles by Arun Shourie, an erudite and skilled journalist, who attempted to show that while there was much oppression of women under Islamic law, the Quran, rightly interpreted, would make possible the removal of the injustices they suffered.[17] Shourie's tone was generous and sympathetic, but he was answered with biting scorn by Rafiq Zakaria, a Muslim and scholar of Islam. Zakaria's criti-

cism was precisely along Kishwar's line: that behind
Shourie's seeming concern for the reform of Islam was
a Hindu contempt for it.[18] Possibly Rajiv Gandhi and
his advisers were shrewder than their many critics gave
them credit for being, and they recognized the need to
attempt a reconciliation with conservative Islamic leaders. Something of this kind of thinking may have been
in Gandhi's mind when he told a delegation of women
opposed to the bill that they should not hold Western
ideas about equality between the sexes.[19]

Two hundred women who had apparently not accepted the prime minister's contention that belief in
equality between the sexes was an un-Indian idea
chained themselves to the gate of Parliament to protest
what they called a black bill meant to appease the fun-
damentalist forces. The bill, however, became law on 6
May, even though perhaps no other piece of legislation
since 1947 had aroused such widespread and impressive
opposition. Most of the English-language press, including papers that normally supported the government,
opposed it. So did women's organizations. So did Muslim lawyers and intellectuals such as A. G. Noorani and
Daniel Latifi and virtually all those referred to in Parliament as "the so-called intelligentsia." The government's
public defense of its case was remarkably poor, consist-
ing largely of the reiteration by the law minister and
others that one had to give the minorities what they demanded. Quite apart from the question of whether the
law was harmful to women's interests, this insistence on
meeting minority demands, even though they ran counter to the general interest of the country, suggests an
acknowledgment that India is not a conventional
nation-state, with laws and customs common to all.

There was another note, however, that ran through

the speeches of the government's supporters during the last day of the debate: reference to "our" laws over and against "theirs." Arun Nehru, the minister of internal security, and one of the most powerful figures in Gandhi's administration, made this distinction, probably quite unconsciously, when he spoke of "our wishes," which included a common legal code, against "the minority community's wishes," implying that he spoke for India while "they" spoke for their community, which was separate from India.[20] "Hindu chauvinism with a liberal face" was the way one commentator described the positions like those of Arun Nehru and Arun Shourie: "They want the Sikhs and Muslims not to create any trouble and they want them to fall in line." But that is not what happens, he went on to say, when a minority feels the majority is trampling on its religious identity: "It rejects the mainstream and creates as much trouble as it can. . . . This is what has happened to the Sikhs and could well happen to the Muslims eventually."[21]

Analysts, both Indian and Western, of Indian politics are inclined to speak of the Muslim problem and the Sikh problem, obscuring the singular importance of the religious commitment of the majority community. This is peculiarly the case when the "we" of political rhetoric collapses their religious and political commitments into a single entity, thereby excluding the "other" from participation in the national identity. It is probably fair to say that the opponents of the Muslim Women Bill, however self-serving they might have been, seemed to understand more clearly than the government the implications for the future of the state of the way that the bill had recognized and defined the claims of a significant religious minority.

6

A Sikh Challenge to the Indian State

Secularism, a much-used word in India, is one of the legacies of the pre-1947 nationalist movement that continues to be interpreted and discussed in relation to the religious and political situation of independent India. The use of the term indicates that despite the numerical superiority of Hindus (eighty-five percent of the population) India is not a Hindu state; that all citizens by constitutional right are free to profess, practice and propagate their religion; that no one will be discriminated against on the basis of religion; that no religion will be favored over another. All of these provisions in the Indian constitution project values of the liberal democratic tradition, which, probably any knowledgeable observer would agree, have been respected by the state and upheld by the courts. But at the same time, the Indian constitution, the legislative bodies, and the courts have involved themselves in the beliefs and practices of religious groups in ways that have led to friction and conflict. The constitution, in article 25, for example, rather offhandedly suggests that Sikhism is a part of Hinduism, which is a statement of little importance to Hindus and one that was not much noticed by Sikhs. When Sikh political autonomy became an issue in the 1980s, however, the innocuous reference became in the eyes of many Sikhs a reflection on the integrity of Sikhism and denial of their rights.

Within the Sikh community there are elements that feel that the linking of Sikhism with Hinduism in the constitution is not just an oversight but a part of a mammoth plot, one that is deliberately engineered by the ruling Hindu majority. In such a situation, grievances that may be economic or political in origin are perceived as coming from a bias against the Sikhs' religious identity, the very core of their being. A reasonable form of action is to respond to the enemies of one's faith with violence, especially when, as is the case of the so-called Sikh extremists, the government is identified with the Hindu majority. When the government uses its power with overwhelming ruthlessness, as it did in the 1984 attack by the army on the Golden Temple, the Sikhs' holiest shrine, its actions are seen as an attack by the Hindus. Furthermore, within the Sikh ethos there is what may be called a theology of martyrdom, not in the Christian sense of a willingness to die rather than abjure one's faith but in the contrary sense of an injunction to fight to the death against the enemies of the faith. All religions have legitimized violence against the wicked and unbelieving, and in Punjab the legitimacy of violence appeared to the extremists to be obvious. The newspapers speak of senseless, random violence, such as the unprovoked shooting of Hindu passengers on buses by the Sikh extremists, and undoubtedly from one angle of vision it is precisely that. But from another angle it is part of a war not of individuals against individuals but of a righteous community against an unrighteous one. In this context, the innocence of an individual caught in the cross fire of war is a regrettable irrelevancy.

With a dreadful monotony, the headlines in recent years have chronicled the skirmishes and intrigues of this war, the killing of bus passengers in Punjab, the murder of politicians and editors, and, no less dreadful, the violence of the police against suspected terrorists, which was how they were always designated in the national press and by the government. In their own literature, they were known as freedom fighters or martyrs. Most of the accounts, except for the identification of the terrorists as Sikhs, gave little if any explanation of the religious component of the violence that has destabilized Punjab for the past six or seven years. The political aspects of the Punjab situation—factions jockeying for power, politicians settling old scores in devious and corrupt ways, the formation of alliances without principles—were all commonplace enough, even if of a stupefying complexity. What was not commonplace in India was the extraordinary level of violence not just on the part of the terrorists but also on the part of the government. "Operation Bluestar," the code name for the army action against the Golden Temple in 1984, killed hundreds more people, many of whom were perhaps guilty only of being Sikhs, just as those whom the terrorists killed were guilty only of being Hindu.

All of this can be, and often is, analyzed without reference to the role of the Sikh religion, but to do so misses much of the inner dynamics and logic of the situation in Punjab. Just as significant, there is scarcely ever, at least in the national press, much analysis of the role of the majority religious community, the Hindus, in relation to the Sikhs. This is one of the ironies of history, for in the popular imagination of both Hindus and Sikhs, Sikhism resulted from its struggle with the Mughal emperors, especially Aurangzeb, who is pictured as the embodiment of Muslim fanaticism. Sikhism, it is stressed, was transformed from a peaceful, pietistic sect into a militant community, fighting battles in which quarter was neither asked for nor given against a powerful government intent on destroying the faithful remnant of believers in the teaching of Guru Nanak. The irony is, of course, that the so-called Sikh terrorists of the 1980s would write these sentences, substituting the government of India for the Mughals and Hindu fanaticism for Muslim fanaticism.

This version of Sikh history is important in considering the implications of the recent Sikh crisis for the future of India's complex religious politics. The ease with which Sikh extremists were able to resort to the language and images of Sikhism to defend their actions invites some fundamental questions. What is Sikhism? Is it the social behavior of a definable caste or regional group? Is it a belief system or a theological statement? And finally, how does the history of Sikhism mesh with other histories: the history of Hinduism, of Islam, of Indian nationalism?

A few years ago, Wilfred Cantwell Smith suggested a moratorium on the use of the word *religion* in academic studies. "Neither religion in general nor any one of the religions," he argued, "is in itself an intelligible entity, a valid object of inquiry or of concern either for the scholar or for the man of faith."[1] While there is no likelihood of this suggestion prevailing over long-established usage, the point should be taken seriously in attempting to define Sikhism or any other Indian religious tradition. The concept of religions as definable entities that can be described both for their own essence and for their effect on society belongs almost entirely to nineteenth-century Western scholarship; the categories associated with the study of religion have been imposed on other cultures by our own.

And yet Smith's advice to adopt a self-denying ordinance abjuring the old categorical terms will not really work. Much of modern humanistic studies and almost all social science use categories formed in the nineteenth century and imposed upon other societies. Too much of the human story has been analyzed in these terms, and to cease using them would weaken our intellectual heritage, even though we can be wary of some of the directions in which it points us. What is necessary, especially in the Indian context, is to be fairly explicit about the particular social, psychological, theological, or political phenomena that are being referred to in a discussion of Sikhism. Otherwise, all terms become convertible, with the political behavior of a particular religious group being ascribed to religion when in fact it can be explained by quite other social causes. The opposite and in some ways more pernicious error to be avoided is the failure to see how religious loyalties may be determining factors in social behavior even though a particular actor may be unaware of it.

Sikhism, like all religious traditions, emerged from and was forged in particular social contexts. Believers within a religious community tend to see the origins of their faith in events and proclamations breaking in from outside time and history. What is involved here is the enormously complex problem of relating religious experience, whatever its validity as "truth," to historical circumstances. J. S. Grewal, the Sikh historian, asserts that the origins of Sikhism must be traced to the response of its founder, Guru Nanak, to the social situation of the Punjab of his time.[2] One might say the same of Martin Luther. But Luther's religious experience might have occurred in many Christian contexts; it is indeed this possibility that makes it relevant to other believers. What is rooted in a particular time and place and could, one suspects, have happened only in the social and historical milieu of the 1520s is the extraordinary response Luther engendered from the German princes. We can say that it was the princes who made the Reformation possible, but that leaves out much of the reality of the events.

We are moving of course, in the realm of the most tired of historical arguments, personality versus historical forces, but persistent questions remain to baffle the scholar, and all answers are ambiguous. Machiavelli phrased the issues in a striking sentence. "It was necessary," he wrote in *The Prince*, "that Moses should find the people of Israel slaves in Egypt and oppressed by the Egyptians, so that they were disposed to follow him in order to escape their servitude."[3] What made for significant change, in this instance and throughout history, Machiavelli asserted, was a congruence of three elements: leadership, fortune (or the accidents of history), and necessity.

The "necessity" of history—the fabric of Punjab society in Guru Nanak's time—and Guru Nanak's influence as a leader interact in the presence of the "accidents" of history, those random events about which we know so little in that period. Analysis of this complex process is particularly important if Guru Nanak was a "founder" of a religion and not merely a reformer. Modern Western scholarship, outside the Sikh community, is inclined to situate Nanak within the general context of Hindu devotional religion, rather than seeing him as a "founder" of a new movement.

Was Nanak's role analogous, on a smaller historical canvas, to that of the Buddha, who is a "founder" in that he is a necessary part of the religious myths that provide a frame for doctrine even though his actual historicity is irrelevant? Or was he like Jesus, whose historical existence is both necessary and relevant for believers even though his actual biography cannot be recovered? Historical studies suggest that Sikhism, like Christianity, is a creation of a believing community and that, while his historicity is unquestioned, Nanak's reality resides in his necessity for the community's faith.

Much of nineteenth-century Indian religious writing appears to be based on Protestant versions of Christian history, especially of the Reformation. When Dayanand Saraswati's followers wanted to exalt their leader, they called him "the Luther of India," and one senses that for many Sikh writers, greatly influenced by the missionary educational patterns that were so strong in the Punjab, Guru Nanak is seen both as a Protestant Jesus and a Protestant Luther. This is a dreary incubus for any historiography, but the selection of Protestant historiography as a model was probably fairly deliberate, or at least it was congenial to the Sikh writers. Roland Robertson argues that Christianity in its Protestant versions "perpetuates the category 'religion' precisely because it has images of how the world ought to be."[4] As N. G. Barrier emphasizes, Sikhism became a "religion" only in the nineteenth century, and this was symbolized by the assertion *hum hindu nahin* (we are not Hindus), an expression of the Sikhs' anxiety to locate their religious

history and hence their own personal identity outside
the Hindu matrix. Barrier's analysis shows how, as he
puts it, a process of sorting and defining boundaries led
to the transformation of old institutions and the creation of new ones.[5]

A fundamental element of religious development in
India in general, and not just in Sikhism, was a concern
of religious communities to state their understanding of
what constituted a good society, "images of how the
world ought to be." The fateful twining of religious leaders' utopian projections with nationalist ideology is a
major theme in the history of nineteenth-century India.
The Sikh vision of a good social and political order is,
as Mark Juergensmeyer suggests, an unregarded component in the modern history of the subcontinent and
understanding it is a task that must be undertaken by
anyone who wants to understand the dynamics of the
Indian situation.[6]

Beyond this is another task, that of relating the Sikh
experience to the Indian context in which it is embedded. Juergensmeyer seems to imply that "Indian civilization" is a misleading term, since in fact it is "a patchwork of regionally specific cultures." This is true, of
course; but this is true also of all great civilizations, including our own. And Indian civilization, like all others,
is a patchwork not just of geographic regions but also of
classes and groups within those regions, with the verti-
cal differences often more significant than the horizon-
tal. England is a classic example of the extraordinary
diversity of class and regional groupings that can be
subsumed under a common political culture in a very
small area. Juergensmeyer's metaphor, however, indicates the historic reality—the patches become a quilt
when the diverse pieces are made to serve a social func-

tion. It is precisely because Indian civilization is a patchwork that, as Juergensmeyer argues, a wider appreciation of the Sikh contribution to Indian history would demonstrate the influence of indigenous and marginal elements in the wider culture.

This is a valid scholarly concern, but in asserting it, two points should be kept in mind. The first is that in making claims for the influence for so-called marginal groups, there should be a continual awareness that in the kind of society in which one marginal group can make a contribution, other marginal groups will also be making contributions. Religious history has been particularly prone to the imbalance and distortion that follow from attempts to prove the importance of sectarian interests. There is, for example, a large bibliography of works to show that everything modern in India, from railways to Radhakrishnan, is due to Christian activity in the nineteenth century. An example from outside India can be found in older writers on the influence of Methodists in eighteenth-century England. They interpreted their success in gaining converts and exercising influence in society as proof of divine intervention. But the same events can be made intelligible to the nonbeliever by reference to the peculiar nature of the English class system working in conjunction with the dislocations and transformations engendered within a rapidly industrializing society.

In India, the Sikhs, by their own choice, are a very visible minority, but for a deeper understanding of how they fit into the interstices of Indian civilization one needs to keep in mind the role of very different kinds of communities, such as the Marwaris. The Marwaris had been a relatively obscure trading caste until the nineteenth century, when many of their members took advantage of the opportunities of the great modern city of Calcutta to establish themselves as dominant figures in Indian industry and banking. One could argue that no other "marginal" element has had such a profound impact on the development of the modern sector of India, but their mode of operation has been very different from that of the Sikhs. Yet it is the same fact—the looseness and toughness of the Indian social fabric—that has made the roles of both groups possible.

This point leads to the second one that must be taken into consideration, that is, the actual historical development of Sikhism in contrast to what may be called the necessary religious myths that nourish the believing community. Barrier has pointed out that Sikhism as it is now embedded in the structural dynamics of North Indian society is largely a product of the historical forces of the nineteenth century. To fit Sikhism into the mainstream of Indian history requires, as Barrier says, "reexamining the myths about what transpired." This would certainly involve a modification of belief in what W. H. McLeod calls "the traditional three stage" interpretation of Sikh history (the work of Guru Nanak as founder, of Arjan as militant organizer, and of Gobind Singh as creator of the Khalsa). McLeod speaks of the need for "a more radical concept of development, one which will express a much more intricate synthesis of a much wider range of historical and sociological phenomena.[7]

The history of Sikhism provides material for a very important contribution to all the grand themes: religion and the rise of capitalism, the relationship between social dislocation and social dynamism, the creative role of minorities, even that grandest of all, the differences between Western and Indian culture. Is there any causal connection between the theological presuppositions of Sikhism and the extraordinary dynamism of Sikhs in the twentieth century? Weber made a careful distinction between the capitalist spirit, or greed, and the spirit of capitalism, *arbeitsethos*, the work ethic, which he believed characterized (not, as his more simplistic interpreters would have it, caused) the transformation of modern western Europe. Is Sikhism, as Weber thought Protestantism was, a self-destroying system, that is, one with an emphasis on individualism and social activity that tends to be destructive of the transcendent elements in religion?

These questions bring us back to the events of the more recent past. In the 1980s a group of Sikhs—mainly young men marginal in many ways to Sikh society as well as to the larger society of India—saw themselves as a saving remnant of the kind that fought the Muslim emperors at Delhi, only now the warfare was against the Hindu central government of India. Nothing is more irrelevant than to say they are only a tiny faction or that most educated, prosperous Sikhs do not agree with them, for saving remnants are by definition few in numbers and marginal to their society. The answer of the violent faction is that of course the majority is not with them. Dulled to true religion, the majority has accepted the arguments and the way of life of the enemies of the faith and by doing so have become enemies of the faith. "Choose ye this day whom ye will serve; as for me and my house we will serve the Lord" is not a saying from the Sikh scriptures, but it summarizes well enough the message, equally simpleminded and self-validating, of Sant Jarnail Singh Bhindranwale, the young religious enthusiast who became the center of the storm of violence in Punjab.

Bhindranwale's brief career and the events that followed after his death in the army action against his followers in the Golden Temple in Amritsar in 1984 are a
paradigm of the way in which an alliance between religion and politics can lead to violence. His family were
poor farmers from an area near Amritsar, known as the
Majha region, that had not shared in the prosperity that
characterizes much of Punjab. The region's people have
a reputation for their devotion to Sikhism, and Bhindranwale was sent as a little boy to a religious school in
the area, the Damdami Taksal, where the emphasis is
on the Sikh scriptures and the traditions and beliefs of
the community. The founder of the school was one of the
heroes of Sikhism, Deep Singh, who in the eighteenth
century died defending the Golden Temple against des-
ecration by the Afghan invader Ahmad Shah Abdali.
The legend of his martyrdom is instructive for understanding the ethos in which Bhindranwale and other
young Sikhs were brought up. Deep Singh's head was
cut off, but he continued for a time to fight against the
Afghans with his head in one hand and his sword in the
other. Pictures and stories of such martyrdoms are common, and while a cult of violence for its own sake was
not inculcated at the Damdami Taksal, the message that
runs through such teaching is that it is necessary to destroy the enemies of the community and that the courage to fight and the willingness to die are essential qualities of the devotee of the Guru.

This point must be emphasized because in India and
elsewhere there is a tendency to argue that the violence
and the murders done in the name of the Sikh community cannot be the work of religious men. From a more
factual point of view, Khushwant Singh, one of the best-
known Sikh writers, argues that the terrorists are either

politically motivated or gangsters.[8] This may be so, but they are undeniably Sikhs, and the fact that they are gangsters in the eyes of the law does not prevent them from being defenders of the faith in their own eyes and, more important, in the eyes of many members of the Sikh community. Long ago it was decided in the Christian Church that the validity of the sacraments did not depend upon the personal morality of the performing priest. In the same way the violence—even the gangsterism—of the terrorist Sikhs does not invalidate their acts in defense of truth. Pacifism is no more a virtue among Sikhs of Bhindranwale's persuasion than it was among the ancient Israelites as they drove out the Canaanites. We have grown accustomed to the idea that warfare is the monopoly of the state, and we forget that for a believing community, whether the Sikhs or the Palestine Liberation Organization (PLO), the highest duty is to preserve itself by whatever means it can. In the late 1930s a young Sikh, Bhagat Singh, was hanged by the government of India for crimes not unlike those in which Sikhs are now engaging in Punjab, and he was praised by Indian nationalists, including Mahatma Gandhi, for his courage and patriotism in acting against the British.

Bhindranwale became a popular preacher and later the head of the Damdami Taksal. This was at the time that Indira Gandhi, who had lost the election in 1977, was seeking new allies for a return to power. In Punjab her opponents were the members of the Akali Dal party, once the spokesmen for Sikh demands for Sikh autonomy but by then fairly conservative. Mrs. Gandhi's people chose Bhindranwale as their ally against the Akali Dal, which he regarded as lacking in enthusiasm for the restoration of Sikhism to its original purity and for Sikh political rights. This gave him and his followers more prominence and influence within the Sikh community and forced the Akalis to more radical positions in order to maintain their credibility as spokesmen for the community.[9]

In India, as elsewhere, when politicians attempt to use a religious group for their own ends they very frequently find that their ally, interested only in its own agenda, may be impossible to control. When Mrs. Gandhi's party, the Indian National Congress, was out of power and Bhindranwale was establishing his own position as a strident critic of the Akalis, he was useful to them. After her party's return to power in 1980, however, Bhindranwale's increasing use of violence, including, it was alleged, murders and robberies for money to support his movement, made even a tacit alliance with him embarrassing. But by then it was difficult for the new government to move against him without weakening its own position in the Punjab by seeming to oppose a religious group identified with reform.

Bhindranwale and his well-armed supporters took possession in 1980 of the Golden Temple in Amritsar, the most important of Sikh holy places, and used it, according to the government, as a center for conducting what amounted to a civil war aimed at the secession of the Punjab from India. Their dream was to establish a state where Sikhs would be free to create a society based on a true understanding of the teachings of their founder, Guru Nanak. Their vision of a good society, their utopia, was in conflict with that of the Indian national state, with its allegiance to secularism. For Bhindranwale, secularism as defined by the Indian government was a thin disguise for Hindu religious and cultural imperialism.

Despite the assassination of many Hindus, as well as Sikhs who were regarded by Bhindranwale as traitors to Sikhism for their support of the government, it was not until 6 June 1986 that the government moved against Bhindranwale's occupation of the Golden Temple. Then with what even many supporters of the government said was unnecessary force, the army invaded the temple, killing hundreds—thousands according to many accounts—including Bhindranwale. Or at least the government produced evidence to show that Bhindranwale had been killed. A group of his followers claimed then that he had not been killed, and they maintain that he is still alive and will lead a new attack on the enemies of the Sikhs. This recalls the belief among the followers of Subhas Chandra Bose, the great Bengali leader who fought against the British in World War II, that he was not killed in an air crash but that he is waiting for the right moment to emerge and lead India to a new day. The leader who lives on beyond death is an ancient and potent religious symbol.

The leadership of the radicals came largely from the All India Sikh Students Federation (AISSF) and students or former students of Bhindranwale's school, the Damdami Taksal. The leaders were far more educated than Bhindranwale and his immediate entourage were, and according to one estimate, ninety percent of the Sikh extremists are college graduates. According to an official of the Golden Temple, many of Bhindranwale's followers had been unemployed, uneducated young men who had little sense of what they were fighting for, but the AISSF was genuinely motivated by religion.[10] What this means is not altogether clear, but it implies that with the loss of the temple as a very visible symbol of their position in the community the radical leaders had to make a more direct appeal through the use of the vocabulary of religion. Killing of Hindus, as well as of Sikhs who were regarded as traitors, once more became commonplace, reaching a spectacular climax with the near assassination of Julio Ribeiro, the head of the Punjab police, inside a highly guarded complex. The investigations showed that the radicals had allies and accomplices among trusted Sikh policemen in the complex, as they had among Mrs. Gandhi's guard at the time of her assassination.

The spokesmen for the radicals after 1984 differed in one very important respect from their predecessors: they declared that they were fighting for Khalistan, a separate homeland for the Sikhs. For some observers, this seemed proof that the movement had become totally political and that it was being financed and encouraged by Pakistan and the Central Intelligence Agency (CIA). Religion, it was argued, had ceased to be a decisive factor in the Punjab situation. But in a curious, convoluted way this argument itself often masked a religious dimension, for it was used by some Hindus to attack Muslims in India who were regarded as friendly to Pakistan, or, in a favorite phrase, as a potential fifth column. As for the demand for Khalistan itself, while the idea of secession might seem purely political, for the Sikhs it surely represented dreams and visions of a homeland of the kind that had made such powerful emotional appeals to Muslims in India before 1947 and, in very different contexts, to Jews in Europe and America. The Sikh policemen who had been in the plot to kill Ribeiro were, by all accounts, very common, not particularly religious, young men, but they explained their actions by saying that Ribeiro was an enemy of the Sikhs, that he "wanted to finish the sons of Guru Gobind

Singh," that is, the followers of the great Sikh leader who had consolidated the Sikhs into a militant religious community. They were joining in the Khalistan liberation forces, they said, because life was not as dear to them as the fight against injustice. The same point was made by Bhai Mohkam Singh, a spokesman for the Damdami Taksal when he was asked why a religious organization such as his was engaged in politics. "Religion and politics go together in Sikhism," he said, "and cannot be separated."[11]

It is not only Sikhs, of course, who declare that religion and politics cannot be separated; so do Christians, Jews, Muslims, Buddhists, Hindus. All the great religions have a vision of what the world should be and how human beings should relate to this vision. It is often said that Hinduism and Islam are not religions but are "ways of life," as if religions are not always ways of life by their very nature. It is because religions are ways of life that they have blueprints for the future, which means that they want a society that is Christian or Islamic or Jewish or Sikh, where they will be able to live the kind of life that permits true fulfillment of religious faith. In the modern world, to want a society that conforms to one's vision of the good life is to want a state to embody that vision, with laws to enforce its pattern against its enemies. It is often said in India, as elsewhere, that those who want their own religious laws and customs to be embodied in the constitution of the state are reactionary and backward, opponents of modernity. This is the frequent charge made against Muslims and Sikhs, but these groups are not defending the past—they are asserting their claims to the future.

In contemporary India, the most important of the groups asserting a claim to the future is neither the

Sikhs nor the Muslims but the Hindus. Here it is scarcely necessary to stress that the Hindus are not, of course, a monolithic unity any more than are the Sikhs and the Muslims. Rather there are groups that speak for what they identify as Hindu interests, or, more ambiguously, as Indian interests. Such groups very frequently speak for the amorphous phenomenon referred to as the "Hindu backlash" against the religious minorities. Stated in its simplest form, this is the belief that the religious minorities have been given concessions that have weakened the fabric of Indian unity. The "backlash" groups vary greatly from each other, and it would be an exaggeration to say that they represent a majority of Hindus. Many observers would agree, however, that in the aggregate they represent a significant demand for the recognition that Indian culture has its roots in the Hindu past and that national unity demands a nationalist ideology based upon it. At one extreme are groups that organize under the name of the Shiv Sena (Army of Shiva), which in Punjab has urged that Hindus must be united in a new militancy against the Sikhs. In Maharashtra, especially in the Bombay area, the original Shiv Sena is a powerful political force. The old Hindu organization Rashtriya Swayamsewak Sangh, or RSS, known for its disciplined cadres pledged to support Hindu dominance, has not been publicly very active. But a new and less openly militant group, the Vishwa Hindu Parishad, has taken a leading part in the campaign to have the Babri Mosque recognized as a Hindu shrine. The support for organizations like the Parishad seems to come largely from the Hindu urban middle class, an indication that the movement reflects the aspirations of many members of this class to see a clear identification of Hinduism with the nation. A more thoughtful expression of the Hindu reaction to the demands of minority religious communities emphasizes the longstanding commitment of Indian political leadership, particularly that represented by Nehru, to the ideal of a secular state, that is, one where all religions are respected but none has a special place. For many members of minority groups, however, this attitude moves inevitably to an identification of national values with Hindu values as it reaches out to encompass others with the dogma that all religions are true. By sheer weight of numbers, a Hindu understanding of the nature and function of religion appears to have become an essential element in nationalist ideology.

No one factor can explain the emergence of religion as a crucial element in politics in India or elsewhere at the end of the twentieth century. Very different processes are at work in Ireland, Iran, Israel, and Lebanon, and only lazy thinking finds a solution in such catch phrases as "the resurgence of fundamentalism." Each country and each region has to be looked at in terms of its historical experience and its own vision of the future.

Almost inevitably in a pluralistic society like India, groups who have a vision of the good society drawn from the religious sources that define their nature and destiny come in conflict with those who have an understanding of their destinies drawn from the experiences and values of other religions. They also come into conflict with those who have a vision of the good society based not on one of the religious communities of India, but on what, for lack of a better term, can be called the secular or liberal democratic tradition. This has found one of its earliest and most elegant statements in the document that declared it to be a self-evident truth that when a political system denied its people the inalienable rights given them by the Creator, that system had to be attacked. This is a revolutionary and radical idea, opening the way for conflict between those with different readings of the intentions of their Creator.

Modern politics in India provide an arena for such conflict in terms of the conventional mechanisms of democracy—voting blocks, parties, and platforms. These platforms, however, often make appeals to voters in the language of religion; the classic example of this is Mahatma Gandhi's use of a religious vocabulary to define an ideology of nationalism. When the democratic process appears unable to satisfy demands that claim to be rooted in religion, violence is the possible and rational solution. Violence in India is not, then, senseless and random. It is a way of changing things, of challenging a recalcitrant political order. In India, as elsewhere in the world at the end of the twentieth century, religions have legitimized violence as people struggle for what they regard as their just claims upon the future. Frustration and fear may have their roots in identifiable economic and social causes which could be ameliorated by secular remedies within the democratic process, but a religious vision can offer a more readily available solution by legitimizing the violence that is born of hatred and despair.

One can sum up the experience in another way: the use of the vocabulary of religion has corrupted political discourse in India and is likely to continue to do so in the immediate future. And, unhappily, this is so in not only India but wherever the vocabulary and vision of a religion is used to institute a social order opposed by groups with equally strong and valid claims upon the future. A conflict of utopias may be the characteristic of our times.

Notes

Chapter 1

1. R. R. Palmer and Joel Colton, *A History of the Modern World* (New York, 1984), p. 145.

2. Wolfgang Friedman, *An Introduction to World Politics* (New York, 1965), p. 16.

3. Thomas O'Dea, *The Sociology of Religion* (Englewood Cliffs, N.J., 1966), p. 4.

4. Ibid., p. 9.

5. Clifford Geertz, *The Interpretation of Cultures* (New York, 1973), p. 112.

6. Unfortunately, there is no literature analyzing the role of religion in Indian society comparable to the seminal studies of the relation of Christianity to Western civilization found in Ernest Troeltsch, *The Social Teachings of the Christian Churches*, trans. Olive Wyon (New York, 1931); H. Richard Niebuhr, *The Social Sources of Denominationalism* (New York, 1929); R. H. Tawney, *Religion and the Rise of Capitalism* (New York, 1947); and Max Weber, *The Protestant Ethic and the Spirit of Protestantism* (New York, 1930).

7. Hans Kohn, "Nationalism," in *International Encyclopedia of the Sciences* (New York, 1968), vol. 10, p. 63.

8. Karl Deutsch, *Politics and Government* (Boston, 1970), p. 80.

9. Michael Barkun, *Disaster and the Millennium* (New Haven, 1974), p. 86.

10. Suzanne Keller, *Beyond the Ruling Class: Strategic Elites in Modern Society* (New York, 1963).

11. Dorwin Cartwright and Alvin Zander, *Group Dynamics: Research and Theory* (Evanston, Ill., 1960), p. 492.

12. O'Dea, *Sociology of Religion*, p. 64.

13. Ibid., p. 64.

14. Karl Mannheim, *Ideology and Utopia*, trans. Louis Wirth and Edward Shils (New York, 1936), p. 192.

15. Ibid.

16. Frederik L. Polak, "Utopia and Cultural Renewal," in *Utopias and Utopian Thought*, ed. Frank E. Manuel (Boston, 1966), p. 290.

17. Manuel, *Utopias*, Introduction.

18. Mircea Eliade, "Paradise and Utopia: Mythical Geography and Eschatology," in *Utopias*, p. 261.

19. Jan Gonda, "Indian Religions," in *The Encyclopedia of Religion*, ed. Mircea Eliade (New York, 1987), vol. 7, p. 169.

20. Mohammad Iqbal, "Presidential Address, 1930," in *Sources of Indian Tradition*, ed. Stephen Hay (New York, 1988), vol. 2, p. 218.

21. Mark Juergensmeyer, "The Logic of Religious Violence: The Case of the Punjab," in *Contributions to Indian Sociology*, n.s., 22, no. 1 (1988).

Chapter 2

1. Jawaharlal Nehru, *Glimpses of World History* (New York, 1942), p. 98.

2. This point is discussed from other perspectives in Rosanne Rocher, *Orientalism, Poetry and the Millennium: The Checkered Life of Nathaniel Brassey Halhead* (Delhi, 1983); Richard Fox Young, *Resistant Hinduism: Sanskrit Sources on Anti-Christian Apologetics in Early Nineteenth-Century India* (Lieden, 1981); and Robert Frykenberg, "The Emergence of Modern 'Hinduism' as a Concept and as an Institution: A Reappraisal with Special Reference to South India," in *Hinduism Reconsidered*, ed. Gunther Sontheimer and Hermann Kulke (Heidelberg, 1988), pp. 1–29.

3. The importance of German thought in interpreting In-

dian culture is detailed in Wilhelm Halbfass, *India and Europe: An Essay in Understanding* (Albany, 1988).

4. Quoted in Raymond Schwab, *The Oriental Renaissance: Europe's Rediscovery of India and the East, 1680–1880* (New York, 1984), p. 429.

5. Quoted in Stephan Koss, *John Morley at the India Office, 1905–1910* (New Haven, 1969), pp. 176–177.

6. Sir Sayyid Ahmad Khan, "Writings and Speeches," in *Sources of Indian Tradition*, ed. Stephen Hay (New York, 1988), pp. 192–195.

7. S. Radhakrishnan, *Eastern Religions and Western Thought* (New York, 1959), pp. 306–313.

8. Barbara S. Miller, trans. *Bhartrihari* (New York, 1967), verse 169.

9. *Bhagavad Gita*, III, 35.

10. Halbfass, *India and Europe*, pp. 172–196.

11. Quoted in Hay, *Sources of Indian Tradition*, p. 31.

12. Quoted in Halbfass, *India and Europe*, pp. 190–191.

13. Nehru, *Glimpses of World History*, p. 736.

14. Nirad Chaudhuri, *The Autobiography of an Unknown Indian* (Berkeley, 1968), p. 195.

15. *The Third Five-Year Plan* (New Delhi, 1961), Introduction.

Chapter 3

1. A. B. Shah, "Religion in Public Life," *Opinion*, 3 September 1968.

2. M. N. Roy, *Fragments of a Prisoner's Diary* (Calcutta, 1950), vol. 1; and Rabindranath Tagore, "The Call of Truth," *Modern Review* 30, no. 4 (1921): 29–33.

3. Gunnar Myrdal, *Asian Drama* (New York, 1968), vol. 1, p. 34.

4. Karl Marx, "The British Rule in India," in *K. Marx and F. Engels: The First Indian War of Independence, 1857–1859* (Moscow, 1959), p. 70.

5. Richard Taylor, "Hindu Religious Values and Family Planning," *Religion and Society*, 16 (1):6–22.

6. A. B. Shah, *Muslim Politics in India*, foreword by Hamid Dalwai (Bombay, 1968).

7. Craig Baxter, *The Jana Sangh* (Philadelphia, 1969), pp. 215–216. Some of the most useful information on the attitudes and activities of the radical right comes from the publications of the Sampradayikta Virodhi Committee, an organization for opposing communalism, and from the publications of the Communist Party of India. The weekly *Organiser* provides insights into the thinking of the Hindu right. It should be read in conjunction with its opposite number from the Muslim radical right, *Radiance*.

8. *Pratap*, 8 December 1968, quoted in M. F. Farooqi, *Communist Party and the Problems of Muslim Minority* (n.p., 1969).

9. Donald Eugene Smith, *India as a Secular State* (Princeton, N.J., 1963), and G. S. Sharma, *Secularism: Its Implications for Law and Life in India* (Bombay, 1966), examine the meaning of the secular state. One of the most interesting examinations of the philosophical implications of the whole question is Frank D. Van Alst, "The Secular State, Secularization, and Secularism," *Quest*, no. 62 (July 1969): 24–35.

10. M. S. Golwalker, "We and Our Nationhood Defined," quoted in Farooqi, *Communist Party and the Problem of the Muslim Minority*, p. 8.

11. A. B. Shah, ed., *Cow Slaughter: Horns of a Dilemma* (Bombay, 1967), offers an analysis of the movement against cow slaughter.

12. Detailed accounts are to be found in the Indian newspapers for April 1969.

13. S. Abid Husain, *The Destiny of Indian Muslims* (London, 1965), p. 129.

14. Joseph Lelyveld, *New York Times*, 28 October 1968.

15. The pamphlet literature of the Jam'at-i-Islami Hind, New Delhi, both in English and Urdu, is considerable, and the materials of the Sampradayikta Virodhi Committee are useful for the Muslim radical right. See, especially, "Introducing the Jam'at-i-Islami Hind" (Delhi, 1966).

16. Mohammad Mujeeb, *The Indian Muslims* (London, 1961), p. 403.

17. Frank Thakur Das, "The Dilemma of the Christians," *Citizen*, 26 July 1969, pp. 14–15.

18. Ibid.

Chapter 4

1. Report of the First Indian National Congress Held at Bombay on 28, 29, and 30 December 1885 (Lucknow, 1886), p. 2.

2. India, Ministry of External Affairs, *Report*, 1971–1972, pp. 73–74.

3. Ibid., p. 76.

4. Ibid.

5. See Subash Kirpekar's article in *The Times Weekly* (Bombay), 29 October 1972, pp. 1–3.

6. Ibid.

7. Selig Harrison, *India: The Most Dangerous Decades* (Princeton, N.J., 1960).

8. The Association for Asian Studies has committees for the regions of India in which members have a special interest, e.g., Bengal, Punjab, Maharashtra. To some Indian officials, this division of committees suggests that American scholars were denying Indian unity and nationhood.

9. John Strachey, *India* (London, 1888), pp. 5–8.

10. Jinnah's letter to Gandhi of 1 January 1940, *Speeches and Writings of Mr. Jinnah*, ed. Jamil ud–din Ahmad (Lahore, 1960), vol. 1, p. 125.

11. A persuasive statement of the argument is given in Rajni Kothari, "Political Reconstruction of Bangladesh: Reflections on Building a New State in the Seventies," *Economic and Political Weekly*, 29 April 1972, pp. 882–885.

12. Ibid., p. 884. Kothari's recent work, *State Against Democracy: In Search of Humane Governance* (New Delhi, 1988), gives a much more pessimistic analysis.

13. Kothari, "Political Reconstruction of Bangladesh," p. 884.

14. Government statistics put the figure much lower, at 3 percent.

15. Francine Frankel, *India's Green Revolution* (Princeton, N.J., 1971), pp. 197–202.

16. Kothari, "Political Reconstruction of Bangladesh," p. 884.

Chapter 5

1. Robert Frykenberg, personal communication with author, May 1989.

2. John Morley, *Indian Speeches (1907–1909)* (London, 1909), speech at Arbroath.

3. Quoted in Dorothy Norman, *Nehru: The First Sixty Years*, (New York, 1965), vol. 1, p. 160.

4. *Alberuni's India*, ed. E. C. Sachau (London, 1914), pp. 20–22.

5. "Chach-Nama," in *The History of India as Told by Its Own Historians*, ed. Sir H. M. Elliot and John Dowson (Allahabad, 1963), vol. 1, p. 184.

6. Sayyid Ahmad Khan, *Monuments of Delhi*, trans. R. Nath (Delhi, 1978).

7. Interview in "Women," *Times of India*, 8 March 1986, p. 5.

8. *Illustrated Weekly of India*, 5 January 1986, p. 56.

9. Arun Shourie, "The Arif Mohammad Affair," *Times of India*, 3 March 1986.

10. *India Today*, 31 January 1986, p. 56.

11. Interview with Hossainur Rahman, *Statesman*, 19 February 1986.

12. Editorial, *Indian Express*, 18 February 1986.

13. Editorial, *Hindustan Times*, 29 March 1986.

14. *Indian Express*, 15 February 1986.

15. *New York Times*, 14 January 1990, p. 3.

16. Madhu Kishwar, "Losing Sight of the Real Issue," *Times of India*, 8 March 1986.

17. Arun Shourie, "The Shariat," *Illustrated Weekly of India*, 2 and 9 March 1986.

18. Rafiq Zakaria, "In Defence of Shariat," *Illustrated Weekly of India*, 2 and 9 March 1986.

19. *India Today*, 31 March 1986, p. 60.

20. "Lok Sabha Passes Muslim Women Bill," *Indian Express*, 6 May 1986.

21. Vir Sangvi, "Hindu Chauvinism with a Liberal Mask," *Sunday Mail*, 6 April 1986.

Chapter 6

1. Wilfred Cantwell Smith, *The Meaning and End of Religion* (New York, 1964), p. 16.

2. J. S. Grewal, "A Perspective on Early Sikh History," in *Sikh Studies: Comparative Perspectives on a Changing Tradition*, ed. Mark Juergensmeyer and N. Gerald Barrier (Berkeley, 1979), p. 35.

3. John Plamenatz, ed., *Machiavelli* (New York, 1975), p. 71.

4. Roland Robertson, *The Sociological Interpretation of Religion* (Oxford, 1970) p. 43.

5. N. Gerald Barrier, "The Role of Ideology and Institution-Building in Modern Sikhism," in *Sikh Studies*, p. 41.

6. Mark Juergensmeyer, "The Forgotten Tradition: Sikhism in the Study of World Religions," in *Sikh Studies*, p. 13.

7. W. H. McLeod, *The Evolution of the Sikh Community* (Oxford, 1976), p. 5.

8. Khushwant Singh, interview in *Expanse*, April 1986.

9. A detailed account of the alliance between Mrs. Gandhi's followers and Bhindranwale is given in Mark Tully and Satish Jacob, *Amritsar: Mrs. Gandhi's Last Battle* (London, 1985), pp. 52–72.

10. Harminder Singh Nanda, "Why Have the Sikhs Taken to Extremism?", *Expanse*, April 1986.

11. Ibid.

INDEX

Compositor: Wilsted & Taylor Publishing Services
Text: 11/14 Aster
Display: Helvetica Condensed
Printer: Thomson-Shore, Inc.
Binder: Thomson-Shore, Inc.